T0156657

MUSIC
Then and Now

Bernie Keating

authorHOUSE®

AuthorHouse™
1663 Liberty Drive
Bloomington, IN 47403
www.authorhouse.com
Phone: 1-800-839-8640

First published by AuthorHouse   11/1/2011

ISBN: 978-1-4670-4040-2 (sc)
ISBN: 978-1-4670-4039-6 (hc)
ISBN: 978-1-4670-4038-9 (e)

Library of Congress Control Number: 2011917242

Printed in the United States of America

Any people depicted in stock imagery provided by Thinkstock are models, and such images are being used for illustrative purposes only. Certain stock imagery © Thinkstock.

This book is printed on acid-free paper.

ALSO BY BERNIE KEATING:

When America Does It Right.
AIIE Press, Atlanta, GA, 1978

Riding the Fence Lines: Riding the Fences That Define the Margins of Religious Tolerance.
BWD Publishing LLC, Toledo, OH, 2003

Buffalo Gap Frontier: Crazy Horse to NoWater to the Roundup.
Pine Hills Press, Sioux Falls, SD, 2008

1960's Decade of Dissent: The Way We Were.
Author House, Bloomington, IN, 2009

Songs and Recipes: For Macho Men Only.
Author House, Bloomington, IN, 2010

Rational Market Economics: A Compass for the Beginning Investor.
Author House Publishing, Bloomington, IN, 2010

Contents

PREFACE

This will be my seventh book with previous ones on economics, religion, and frontier history, plus a novel. I do not claim expertise on any of these subjects, but that did not prevent me from writing about them based on research and my own insights. This new book will be about music -- among other things such as art and architecture.

I am not a musician; however, as a young boy during the Great Depression, my favorite hour of the week was when John Charles Thomas sang on *KOBH*, the only radio station we received in Buffalo Gap. Music has always lifted me up to the best-of-times.

When listening to Elton John's music in the Lion King, I feel re-connected to my aboriginal roots. A rhythmic beat has remained the same whether it was early man striking two sticks together, a Mozart symphony, or Mick Jagger on center stage at a rock concert. Music moved from a lyre in Ancient Greece to a motet in the 13th century, and eight hundred years later to Glen Miller's swing in the 20th.

As we look at the music of an era, we must consider the conditions under which the people lived; music reflects the environment. That was true a thousand years ago and remains the same today.

It is not fair to compare people from different eras -- but I will anyway. Beethoven could not have composed a masterpiece any better than George Gershwin's *Rhapsody in Blue*. Yes, they are from different eras with different tastes, but Gershwin was also a genius. Has any music been more relevant to our generation than that of Frank Sinatra,

Ray Charles, the Beatles, Elvis, and Carry Underwood? We have *jazz, swing, rock'n'roll*, and *country*; each loved by their own sub-culture. What will be the mainstay of musical taste in fifty years -- or even another ten?

Please join me as I travel through time with Wolfgang Amadeus Mozart, George Gershwin, the Beatles, Elvis, and Elton John. I had fun doing the research and writing the book, and I hope you enjoy it.

Bernie Keating

ONE: WHY MUSIC?

Elton John is a superstar; I got wondering how he compares to Wolfgang Amadeus Mozart, a superstar of his era. Or how about the comparison of my favorite musical, *The Music Man*, with my favorite opera, *La boheme*, composed by Giacomo Puccini over a hundred years ago?

What is the pull of music? Why do we tap our foot to a beat or love a favorite melody? It goes way back; music has been a part of the human experience since earliest times. Native people danced to a rhythm and millenniums later this grew into the *ballets* of Tchaikovsky, *swing* of Glenn Miller, and *rock'n'roll* of Elvis.

Why music? Even though it is elusive, music is the most direct means we have to communicate -- a force since the first person raised their voice in song. Today, it blares or whispers at us from a thousand venues. Music is puzzling even to those who create it; rhythm seems to control the speed of life and melody has been dissected, but nobody has unraveled the secret of its impact -- all we can say is "a melody is a row of notes tautly and loosely related, depending on the width of intervals and its speed, whether by instrument or the human voice." [1]

Psychologists cannot explain why we love -- or dislike -- a particular genre or why it has such an impact on our psyche -- those things we hear such as melody, phrasing, harmony, rhythm, or quasi-linguistic elements such as syntax. [2] Psychology comes into play: tugging at the heart, music first tickles the neurons. The following is an interview with Paul Simon. He was rehearsing his song, *Darling Lorraine*, which is about a love that starts hot but turns very cold. He found himself thinking about a three-note rhythmic pattern near the end, and said:

> *"The song has this Tripler going on underneath that pushes it along, and at a certain point I want it to stop because the story suddenly turns very serious. The stopping of sounds and rhythms, it's really important, because how can I miss you unless you're gone? If you just keep the thing going like a loop, eventually it loses its power."* [3]

I'm not sure I understood what he was talking about, but apparently it worked, because he created a great song.

Some basics have remained the same from Bach to the Beatles; yet we have also seen enormous change as one style of music changed to another. Let's take a brief look at our modern music that began with *jazz*.

Jazz started with Black slaves who brought their musical heritage from Africa that found expression in "work songs" and "field hollars" of the American South. Then it moved into the saloons and bordellos of New Orleans. Louis Armstrong was a pioneer in the 1920's; Paul Whiteman's orchestra performed George Gershwin's *Rhapsody in Blue*, a sophisticated composition of *jazz*; and Duke Ellington opened in 1927 at New York City's Cotton Club -- and *jazz* became a new musical genre. Later in the 1930's, a sub-genre called *swing* developed that had a smoother rhythm and more sophisticated melodies. Big Bands reigned supreme with bandleaders:

> Benny Goodman, Duke Ellington, Count Basie, Glenn Miller, Harry James, Louis Armstrong, Artie Shaw, Cab Calloway, Tom and Jimmy Dorsey, Fletcher Henderson, Gene Krupa, Gloria Parker and her *All Girl Orchestra*, Louis Prima, Les Brown, Dave Brubeck, Stan Kenton, Woody Herman, Fats Waller, Tex Beneke, and Lawrence Welk.

In following decades, other sub -genre appeared including *boogie woogie*, and the *jitterbug*. Vocalists became popular:

Bing Crosby, Ella Fitzgerald, Nat King Cole, Rosemary Clooney, Frank Sinatra, Tony Bennett, Neil Diamond, Doris Day, Aretha Franklin, the Andrew Sisters, Patti Page, the McGuire Sisters, and a host of others who filled the airways of radio and TV.

The times saw *rock'n'roll* and *rhythm & blues*. They grew with synergy: *rock'n'roll* was influenced by *rhythm & blues* and drew on *jazz* and *classical*. Elvis Presley opened the door in 1954 with his single *That's All Right (Mama)*, followed by *Shake, Rattle, and Roll*. Other artists included Little Richard and Jerry Lee Lewis, soon followed by Eddie Fisher, Perry Como, and Patti Page.

The Beach Boys started in Southern California with *Fun, Fun, Fun* and followed with *California Girls*. The Beatles made an appearance on the Ed Sullivan TV show, and their hit song *I Want to Hold Your Hand* was on *Billboard* for months. Superstars such as Mick Jagger, Bruce Springsteen, Elton John, Barry Manilow, Stevie Wonder, and Sting toured world-wide filling stadiums with concerts. *Country* music came principally from the Grand Ole Opera in Nashville, and *sacred* music from the "Bible Belt".

Why Music? Humans have pursued it from earliest times. Let's start at the beginning and follow music through its long evolution.

TWO: EARLY HISTORY OF MUSIC AND ART

We can only surmise the nature and sound of music by early man, but during my youth I witnessed how it might have sounded when Sioux Indians from a nearby reservation performed their traditional native dances in Buffalo Gap. Beating on rawhide leather drums, the men chanted "hi yaw, hi yaw, hi yaw," while other warriors brandishing spears, pranced around a fire while their women danced with a heel-toe beat. All wore colorful costumes and jewelry crafted from animals in their local environment. That scene during my youth in the 1930's could, perhaps, be symbolic of how man celebrated music and the arts during the early times.

No one is certain what earliest music was like. We are not even sure how Bach's orchestra sounded, only ten generations ago. But we can be sure that primitive man discovered rhythms from the movements of their bodies and melody from the changing pitch of their own voices. When they recognized the power of these elements of music, they them made them tools of communication, incantation, sorcery and enjoyment. [4]

Music is found in every known culture, past and present. Around 50,000 years ago, early humans began to disperse from Africa, reaching all the habitable continents. Since all people have some form of music, scientists conclude that it is likely to have been present in the ancestral population prior to the dispersal of humans around the world. Consequently, it has been in existence for a long time and the first music evolved to become a fundamental constituent of human life. [5]

In the 10th millennium B.C., the Neolithic [6] man learned to produce food rather than collect it -- the beginning of agriculture; communities come into being, laying the foundation for civilizations that will follow. Art objects date from the 7th millennium B.C. that are figurines of animals and humans made from finely carved bone or ivory. Reliefs of humans or animals are carved on rock walls and the most spectacular are the paintings dominated by large animals such as mammoth, horse, or bison; the precise meaning is impossible to recover, but appears to have played a part in group ceremonial activity. Human developments during the Ice Age included an increased awareness of individual and group identity and a new field of artistic activity. [7]

During our travels, my wife and I visited Neolithic ruins near Rahal Gdid in Ireland, the Stonehedges of England, and other ruins on Malta. Anthropologists know from artifacts and construction at these sites that early man was inspired by religion and were artists, architects and astronomers. It is almost certain that they also developed their own form of primitive music -- civilization moved forward.

THREE: THE GREEK CULTURE OF ART AND MUSIC

Greek was the language of Homer and Athenian philosophers and it holds an important place in the history of the Western World. The New Testament was written in Greek; liturgies continue to be celebrated in the language in various Christian denominations.

In 3000 B.C., Greek civilization began to flourish: the Minoans who lived on the island of Crete were Europe's first advanced civilization. A thousand years later, the island is struck by a two-hundred foot tsunami, destroying their civilization and making way for the rise of the mainland Greek Mycenaeans. Greek civilization reaches its height in 400 B.C. -- called the Hellenic Age, and Socrates lays the foundation for Western thought. *Alexandra the Great* amasses an empire that stretches from Egypt to India, spreading Greek ideas and customs. The culture of Greece evolved over thousands of years, through the Roman Empire and then to its Eastern successor, the Byzantine Empire. Foreign occupiers such as the Medieval Latin Kingdoms, Venetian Republic, Genoese Republic, British Empire, and Ottoman Empire have left their influence on Greek culture. Because of the ravages of time, only a minor assortment of ancient Greek art has survived -- frequently in the form of sculpture and architecture. [8]

In Ancient Greece, "music was both a part of everyday life and a manifestation of the divine ... no God ranked higher than the music God, Apollo, and no artist-hero was as popular as Orpheus with his heart-shaped lyre. The Greeks held annual Olympiads of music that had the status of a World Series, and a virtuoso on the reed-pipes or the lyre was the equivalent of a modern home-run king. The Greek, Pythagoras, discovered the relationship between the length of a vibrating string, or a column of air, and the pitch it produced. He continued with the discovery of harmonics. ... Disciples of Pythagoras found there were natural acoustical strong points, notably the fourth and fifth notes within an octave. ... But although we know something about Greek Theories, we know nothing of how their music sounded." [9]

Architecture was nonexistent in Greece from the end of the Mycenaean period to the 7th century B.C. when plebeian life and prosperity recovered to a point where public building could be undertaken. During the Greek Classic period -- 400's B.C. -- Greek painting, sculptures, and architecture were not "art-for-art sake" in the modern sense. The architect was only a craftsman employed by the state. "No distinction was made between the architect and the building contractor. The architect designed the building, hired the laborers and craftsmen who built it, and was responsible for the budget and timely completion. He did not enjoy any of the lofty status accorded to modern architects of public buildings. An architect like Iktiinos, who designed the Parthenon, would today be seen as a genius but was treated in his lifetime as no more than a very valuable master tradesman." [10]

There were three order styles in Greek architecture: Doric, Corinthian, and Ionic. These names reflected their belief that the styles descended from the ancient Dorian and Ionian Greeks.

Most surviving Greek buildings such as the Parthenon on the Acropolis are Doric. This style was used in mainland Greece and spread from there to the Greek colonies in Italy. It was more formal and austere; the Ionic was more relaxed and decorative. The small temple of Athena Nike on the Acropolis is Ionic. This style was used in the cities of Ionia (Ephesus on the west coast of Turkey) and some of the Aegean islands. The ornate Corinthian style was a later development. While elaborate, it was used mostly on smaller works, like the monument to Lysicrates at Athens. [11]

Delphi, a several hour drive north of Athens is a must-see. This legendary place speaks for itself as the most important shrine of Greece when it was the center of the world. In mythology, Delphi was the site of the Delphic oracle, and a major site for the worship of the god Apollo. Starting in 586 B.C., athletes from all over the Greek world competed in the Pythian Games, a predecessor to our modern Olympic games.

My wife and I have had the opportunity to visit many of the sites with our Greek son-in-law as tour guide. Our oldest daughter, during her career as a naval officer, married George when she was stationed at the U.S. Naval Communication Station in Nea Makri near Athens. He became a naturalized American citizen, but they have maintained a second home in Rafina, Greece, near his family. We traveled with them with a unique experience to view first-hand the ancient architecture and culture.

FOUR: HOMER

Ὅμηρος Homēros

Homer is the author of the Iliad and the Odyssey, and is revered as the greatest ancient Greek poet. His epics, along with other things he brought such as music, are at the beginning of Western culture and have had an enormous influence since earliest times. When Homer lived is controversial because it came before historical records. Some estimate he lived around 850 B.C., while others claim that he lived much nearer to the time of the Trojan War in the early 12th Century B.C. The poems are generally seen as the culmination of many generations of oral story-telling. Some scholars claim that "Homer" is a fictitious or constructed name, but the influence of the Homeric epics in shaping Greek culture is widely recognized. Regardless of the inexact date, he lived in ancient Greece and had a profound influence on the culture of Western civilization.

"Homer" is a Greek name, and although nothing definite is known about him, traditions arose giving details of his birthplace and background. He is said to be born in the Ionian region of Asia Minor at Smyrna, or on the island of Chios. Evidence from the poems gives a familiarity with the topography and place-names of this region. The poet's name is interpreted by some as meaning "he who accompanies; he who is forced to follow", or in some dialects, "blind". This led to many tales that he was a blind man, which may have arisen from the meaning of the word in Ionic and Aeolian. The characterization of

Homer as a blind bard goes back to some verses that recount stories of Troy to the shipwrecked Odysseus. [12]

Other scholars take the name of the poet to mean "he who fits (the Song) together". A related verb can mean "sing". Some think that "Homer" may have meant "he who puts the voice in tune" with dancing, and argue that the name is the echo of an archaic word for "reunion", denoting a formal assembly of competing minstrels. Some depict Homer as a wandering minstrel. [13]

As an overview, we are given the image of a "blind, begging singer who hangs around with little people: shoemakers, fisherman, potters, sailors, elderly men in the gathering places of harbour towns".

I am not a historian, so I can voice my own opinion. I think Homer was re-incarnated in our lifetime, and was really Elvis Presley in disguise.

FIVE: ROMAN CULTURE OF ART AND MUSIC

I can discuss the Architecture of Ancient Rome as someone who has visited it numerous times. During a previous working career, I was the Corporate Manager of Quality Assurance for the multi-national company, Owens Illinois, which was the world's largest producer of glass, plus other packaging materials. In a role as consultant to our International Division, I travelled extensively to assist our overseas affiliates with quality issues. That took me to Italy where our affiliate owned virtually all of the Italian glass industry; so I visited every part of the country, working in factories during weekdays and sight-seeing on weekends in the company of local tour guides.

The Romans eventually overcame the Greek Empire. We know little about Roman music. There are a number of partially extant sources on the music of the Greeks; however, very little survives about the music of the Romans. There are various reasons for this, one of which is that early Roman fathers of the Christian church were aghast at the music of theatre, festivals, and pagan religion and suppressed it once Christianity became the official religion of the Roman Empire under Emperor Constantine.

"The Romans were not particularly creative or original when it came to music. They did not attach any spiritual *ethos* to music, as did the Greeks. Yet, if the Romans admired Greek music as much as they admired everything else about Greek culture, it is safe to say that Roman music was mostly monophonic -- single melodies with no harmony. The rhythm of vocal music may have followed the natural metre of the lyrics." [14]

Rome adopted Greek architecture and then created a new Roman style. They were also indebted to their Etruscan forefathers who supplied them with a wealth of knowledge essential for solutions such as hydraulics and the construction or arches. Architecture flourished throughout the empire during the *Pax Romana*. [15] The architectural highlights of Rome are the Forum and the Coliseum. [16] High population in cities forced the Romans to discover new architectural solutions. The use of vaults and arches together with a sound knowledge of building materials enabled them to achieve unprecedented success in the construction of imposing structures. Examples include the Aqueducts of Rome, Baths of Diocletian, and the Coliseum. These were reproduced on a smaller scale in other towns of the empire.

The Ancient Romans intended that public buildings should be made to impress as well as perform a public function. The Pantheon is a supreme example of this, particularly in the version rebuilt by Hadrian, which remains perfectly preserved, and which over the centuries has served as the inspiration for countless public buildings. Hadrian also left his mark on the landscape of northern Britain when he built a wall to mark the northern limits of the Roman Empire: Hadrian's Wall. [17]

The Romans based much of their architecture on the dome, such as Hadrian's Pantheon and the Baths of Diocletian. It permitted construction of vaulted ceilings and provided large covered public space such as the public baths and basilicas. The Roman use of the arch facilitated the building of many aqueducts throughout the empire, such as the magnificent Aqueduct of Segovia and the eleven aqueducts in Rome. The same idea produced numerous bridges, which are still used. An arch is a strong shape as no single spot holds all the weight; it is still used in architecture today. The Triumphal Arch became a symbol of power and was utilized within Christian basilicas to symbolize the triumph of Christ and the afterlife. [18]

The major forms of Roman art are sculpture and mosaic work. Artists often copied Greek precedents and much of the Greek sculpture known today is in the form of Roman marble copies. But some Roman art is highly creative, relying on Greek models but also encompassing Etruscan, native Italian, and even Egyptian visual culture. Pliny, Ancient Rome's most important historian, recorded that nearly all the forms of Roman art came from Greece. The high number of Roman copies speaks of the esteem Roman artist had for Greek art. When Constantine moved the capital of the Roman Empire to Byzantium (renamed Constantinople and later Istanbul), art incorporated Eastern influences to produce the Byzantine style. Rome was sacked in the 5th century, and artisans moved to the Eastern capital. The Church of Hagia Sophia in Constantinople became a final burst of Roman art.

Historians, with hindsight, have given names to various periods of history. We will start in Chapter Six with the *Romanesque* period that followed the collapse of the Roman Empire.

SIX: ROMANESQUE PERIOD

Romanesque is the era that followed the collapse of the Roman Empire. "Collapse" is a mild term to describe the chaos during the centuries after the Empire suffered defeats that began at the hands of the Goths. The Goths were barbaric tribes that roamed in present-day Germany north of the Danube River that formed the boundary with the Roman Empire. When the Danube froze in 276 A.D., the Goths crossed it and began raids on the Empire, hastening its crumpling and demise. The Vandals, a people closely kindred to the Goths, also crossed the Danube and began raids. The Huns from further east in present-day Russia then also began to make conquests over portions of the Empire. In 493 A.D., a Goth became King of Rome, but already for seventeen years there had been no Roman Emperor. So it was in this utter social decay and collapse that ... Rome came to an End. [19]

Western Europe was a chattered civilization without law, without administration, with roads destroyed and education disorganized -- a time of confusion, of brigandage, of crimes unpunished and universal insecurity. It is interesting to trace how, out of this universal melee, the beginnings of a new order began to develop during the following centuries. [20]

In was in the aftermath of this collapse of the Roman Empire that the *Romanesque* Period in history began. Romanesque architecture was the first creative art to emerge in about 1000 A.D. The most striking advances were made in France, but the style was developed in all parts of Europe. It resulted from the great expansion of monasticism in the 10th and 11th centuries, when Europe first regained a measure of political stability after the fall of the Roman Empire. [21]

Romanesque architecture was the first distinctive style to spread across Medieval Europe. It is known by its massive quality, thick walls, round arches, sturdy piers, groin vaults, large towers and decorative arcading. The buildings have clearly defined forms and are frequently of regular, symmetrical plan so that the overall appearance is one of simplicity when compared with gothic buildings that were to follow.

Many castles were built during this period, but they are greatly outnumbered by churches. The most significant are the great abbey churches, a few of which are still standing, more or less complete and frequently in use; however, many were partly or entirely rebuilt in the later Gothic period.

The Dark Ages were perhaps the most turbulent time in world history. Muhammad founded the Islamic religion in the 6th century and his Muslim Empire later stretched from the east in Indonesia, through the Middle East, across North Africa, and to Spain. During seven hundred years until the 14th century, the Iberian Peninsula (Spain) was Muslim territory.

The greatest building of the *Romanesque* Dark Ages, Emperor Charlemagne's Palatine Chapel, Germany, was built in 800 A.D., when Charlemagne was crowned ruler of the Holy Roman Empire, a loose confederation of German and Italian states. After his death in 814 A.D., the empire collapsed.

This was the era when Europe was affected by a feudal system established as a way of organizing and protecting communities. Peasants held tenure from local rulers over the land that they farmed in exchange for military service. They could be called upon, not only for local and regional spats, but to follow their lord to travel across Europe to the Crusades if they were required to do so. The Crusades, 1095-1270 A.D., were a series of religious wars of Christians against Muslims who occupied the Holy Land. One of the effects of the Crusades, which were intended to wrest the Holy Land of Palestine from Islamic control, was to excite a great deal of religious fervor, which in turn inspired building programs. "The Nobility, upon safe return, thanked God by the building of a new church." [22]

The system of monasticism, in which the religious become members of an order with common ties and a common rule, was established by the monk Benedict in the 6th century. The Benedictine Monasteries spread from Italy throughout Europe. The monasteries, which sometimes also functioned as cathedrals, were a major source of power; bishops lived and functioned like princes. The monasteries were the seats of learning of all sorts, and Benedict ordered that all the arts were to be taught.

The invasion of England by William, Duke of Normandy, in 1066 A.D., saw the building of castles that reinforced the Norman presence. Several churches that were built at this time were founded by rulers as seats of temporal and religious power. These include the Abbaye-Saint-Denis, Speyer Cathedral, and Westminster Abbey (where little of the Norman church now remains)." [23]

Can you imagine what it was to live within the *Romanesque* environment? While musical life may have been rich, it is hard to imagine how peasants found the inspiration to sing. The only repertory of music which has survived from before 800 A.D. to the present day is the liturgical music of the Roman Catholic Church, the largest part of which are called Gregorian Chants. In the sixth century, Pope Gregory decreed that it should be written down and codified; for the next 1000 years these severe-sounding unisons of the Gregorian Chants were the basis of all Catholic services, and the Mass was the fundamental source of all medieval lyrics. [24]

As with architecture during this period, church music also became massive, but the music of these early Christian centuries was devout rather than elaborate. Secular music was prohibited by the church. Antiphonic music was common (Scriptural verse sung as part of the liturgy). The congregation sang songs in unison, for as yet part-singing had not been devised. Music was a great outlet for suppressed emotions, but was in a state of chaos. "There was no regular meter, no bar lines, no established scales, and at a time when music was still primarily vocal, there was not even a stable language to sing in: Latin was disintegrating and the Romanic Languages -- Italian, Spanish, and French -- had not yet become fixed." [25]

As monasticism spread across Europe, *Romanesque* churches sprang up in France, England, Scandinavia, Poland, Hungry, Sicily, Serbia, Tunisia, and elsewhere. The *Romanesque* style gradually transitioned into the *Gothic* period; however, the term did not exist during the years it actually developed and was applied in hindsight by historians many centuries later.

During our travels in Europe, my wife and I visited *Romanesque* architecture in such buildings as the Cathedral of Lisbon, Portugal; Santa Maria in Cosmedin, Rome; the Baptistery in Florence, Italy; Abbey Les Hommes in Caen, France; and Mont Saint-Michel, France.

SEVEN: GOTHIC PERIOD

Gothic is the second era that flourished in Europe during the Middle Ages. It evolved from *Romanesque* and lasted from the 12th to the 16th century. The term *"Gothic"* was coined in hindsight by writers of the Renaissance, who attributed the medieval architecture to the barbarian Gothic tribes that had destroyed the Roman Empire. The term retained its derogatory overtones until the 19th century, at which time a positive revaluation of Gothic architecture took place. Although modern scholars have long realized that Gothic art has nothing in truth to do with the Goths, the term remains a standard in the study of history.

Architecture was the most important art form during the Gothic period. Its principal characteristics are the means to support ceiling vaults over wide spans. The stonework of the traditional church vault exerted a downward and outward pressure that tended to push the walls outward, thus collapsing them. Supporting walls had to be made extremely thick. Since the vault was carried at discrete points, piers could replace the continuous thick walls. The round arches were replaced by pointed arches, which distributed thrust downward from the top. The outward thrust of the ceiling was carried to a flying buttress, which supported the ceiling. These elements enabled masons to build taller buildings than their predecessors. The skillful use of flying buttresses made it possible to build tall, thin-walled buildings whose interior structural system of piers and ribs reinforced an impression of soaring verticality. [26]

The earliest surviving *Gothic* building was the abbey of Saint-Denis in Paris, begun in about 1140 A.D. Notre-Dame de Paris followed in 1165 A.D. The basic form of *Gothic* architecture eventually spread throughout Europe. In England, it had its own particular character that was epitomized by Salisbury Cathedral. English *Gothic* churches had thicker walls, sparing use of tall windows, and piers of a central column of stone surrounded by a number of slimmer columns made of marble. [27] (My wife and I visited all three of these cathedrals)

As previously mentioned, *Gothic* does not imply architecture of the Goths; it has a much wider application. "The term originated as a pejorative description that was used to describe culture that was considered rude and barbaric. Italy had overturned a culture that was almost entirely focused on the Church, which was perceived by many as a period of ignorance and superstition. *Goth* was the equivalent of *vandal*, a savage despoiler with a Germanic heritage, and was applied to the architectural styles of northern Europe." [28]

At the end of the 12th century, Europe was divided into a multitude of city states and kingdoms. The northern area encompassing Germany, Netherlands, Belgium, Luxemburg, Switzerland, Austria, eastern France and northern Italy was nominally part of the Holy Roman Empire. The southern area of France, Portugal, Scotland, Spain, and Sicily were independent kingdoms. [29]

The early medieval period had seen a rapid growth in monasticism with several orders spreading their influence widely. Foremost were the Benedictines whose abbey churches vastly outnumbered any others. St Francis of Assisi established the Franciscans, and the Dominicans were founded in the same period by St. Dominic. These two religious orders were particularly influential in the building of Italy's churches.

In the 1200's, Genghis Khan amassed his empire in the East. He came out of Mongolia to run rampant and the Mongol Empire became the largest contiguous in history, which included much of Eastern Europe, Russia, and the Middle East. His campaigns resulted in the deaths of 40 million people. Following this tumult, in the 1300's the

Black Death (bubonic plague) became the most devastating pandemic in human history; it is estimated to have killed 30% to 60% of Europe's population. This created a series of religious, social, and economic upheavals that had profound effects on the course of European history, and it took 150 years for Europe's population to recover.

Slowly, music began to see some change. The age of polyphony (combining two or more voices) was beginning in the eighth century, and men began to sing different tunes simultaneously. Martin Luther, centuries later in describing a piece of polyphony, wrote:

> *"Is it not remarkable and admirable that one voice can sing a simple tune while three or four others, singing along, joyfully enfold this simple tune, playing and leaping around and embellishing it wonderfully, skillfully as if they were leading a heavenly dance, meeting and embracing each other amiably and cordially."*

These were the sturdy, simple, even severe tunes that were the antithesis of counterpoint. They were to establish congregational singing and to become a focus of the early Protestant movement. [30]

During the 13th, 14th, and 15th centuries, a popular form of music was the motet, a song in which one voice, the tenor, sang a narrow melody while two or three others spread their voices around, sometimes in several different languages at once. Song was flourishing in taverns and castles, on village greens and squares -- everywhere outside the restrictive walls of the Church. Composers became fascinated by classical stories and improved the words by means of music, probing to find the musical phrase that would best express a line of poetry. One of their most popular forms was the madrigal, a four-voice composition that made use of a large chorus. The finest madrigals were cunningly devised so that a key word or phrase -- often amorous or naughty -- would suddenly stand out in the sonorous web of counterpoint like a patch of blue showing through a cloudy sky -- and then the busy, often jolly counterpoint would close in again. "English madrigals playfully imitated natural sounds, notably the call of the cuckoo." [31]

One of the most important English composers was William Byrd, a great madrigalist in the 1600's. He is often credited with the invention of the solo song, which he set to lute accompaniment, or which he wrote to be sung in stage plays, thus foreshadowing in concept the Italian opera. [32]

I personally encountered my first *Gothic* cathedral during a consulting trip to a glass factory my company owned in Seville, Spain. The cathedral had the typical flying buttress on both sides, but I had difficulty in understanding the strange interior layout. A local tour guide then explained that this was originally an Islamic mosque when Muslims occupied Spain. After the Christians drove them out, they converted the mosque into a Roman Catholic cathedral with a new roof and the flying buttresses, but did little with the interior layout; so it did not have the traditional *Gothic* architectural style of other European cathedrals.

As a tourist traveling through Europe, my wife and I encountered *Gothic* cathedrals in virtually all the major cities. The cathedral in Reims, France, was one of the earliest built and my favorite. It was heavily damaged during both World Wars and rebuilt with funds from the Rockefeller Foundation. Other *Gothic* cathedrals of particular note are Notre Dame in Paris, cathedral in Cologne, cathedral in Milan, and Salisbury cathedral in England.

In the next chapter we will look at the *Byzantine* era that overlapped with other periods and occurred in a different part of the world.

EIGHT: BYZANTINE ART AND ARCHECTURE

After the fall of Rome in 476 A.D. marking the end of the West Roman Empire, the East Roman Empire that had remained Christian (Eastern Orthodox religion) but had been significantly influenced by the East, survived as the *Byzantine Empire* and was centered in Constantinople. It existed for a thousand years and during its existence it was one of the most powerful economic, cultural, and military forces in Europe. After 1071 A.D., however, much of the empire's homeland in Asia Minor was lost to the Seljuk Turks. It received a mortal blow in 1204 A.D. from the Fourth Crusade, when it was dissolved and divided into competing Greek and Latin realms. Its territories were lost with the Fall of Constantinople and the cession of remaining territories to the Muslim Ottoman Empire in the 15th century. [33]

Byzantine architecture gradually emerged as a distinct artistic style when Emperor Constantine moved the capital of the Roman Empire from Rome to Byzantium, which was renamed Constantinople and is now called Istanbul. Following the capture of Constantinople by the Ottoman Turks in 1453 A.D., it became the Ottoman Empire. [34]

In *Byzantine* architecture, a distinct style imposed certain influences from the Near East: buildings increased in geometric complexity, classical Ionic and Doric orders were used, mosaics replaced carved decoration, complex domes rested on massive piers, and windows filtered light through thin sheets of alabaster to softly illuminate interiors. "Prime examples of early *Byzantine* architecture date from Justinian's reign and survive in Ravenna and Istanbul. One of the breakthroughs in architecture occurred in the 7th century when Justinian's architects invented a system providing for a smooth transition from a square plan of the church to a circular dome by means of squinches or pendentives." [35]

There are many examples of Byzantine architecture in Russia. Saint Basils Cathedral in the Red Square in Moscow and Saint Isaac Cathedral in Saint Petersburg are prime examples. We have an oil painting on our wall of the "Church of The Sacred Blood" that we purchased in Saint Petersburg during a tour.

Byzantine art developed out of the art of the Roman Empire. The most salient feature was its abstract character. Classical art attempted to mimic reality as closely as possible, but *Byzantine* art abandoned this in favor of a more symbolic approach. The cause of this transformation, which largely took place during late antiquity, has been a subject of scholarly debate for centuries. [36]

The *Byzantine Empire* gradually lost its territories to the Muslims, and was overtaken by the Ottoman Empire while the *Renaissance* took place elsewhere in Europe.

NINE: THE RENAISSANCE:

Scholars have spent entire careers doing research and writing books about the *Renaissance,* so I am a midget standing in the shadow of giants; however, perhaps I can bring a new sense of organization to this complex period.

Renaissance means literally "rebirth," the period in European civilization following the Middle Ages characterized by a surge of interest in classical learning and values. The *Renaissance* also witnessed the discovery and exploration of new continents, the substitution of Copernican for the Ptolemaic system of astronomy, the decline of the feudal system, the growth of commerce, and the invention of such potentially powerful innovations as paper, printing, the mariner's compass, and gunpowder. To the scholars and thinkers of the day, however, it was primarily a time of the revival of classical learning and wisdom after a long period of cultural decline and stagnation. [37]

Like so much of history, the *Renaissance* began in the backwater of disconnected events. The end of the Middle Ages set in motion a series of social, political, and intellectual reforms that culminated in the *Renaissance.* These were the result of increasing failure of the Roman Catholic Church to provide a framework for spiritual and material life, the rise of city-states, the development of national languages, and the breakup of the old feudal structures. During the Dark Ages, society in most of Europe was rigorously controlled by the Roman Catholic Church. This included the era of the "Spanish Inquisition" when heretics were burned at the stake, which stifled dissent and impeded social progress. For several centuries Muslims controlled all of North Africa, the Middle East, and most of Spain; they were finally pushed out of Spain in the 1400's. In the year 1492, you may remember from a poem

"In fourteen hundred and ninety two,
Columbus sailed the ocean blue."

And he "discovered" America during the realm of Queen Elizabeth of Spain. This was an era of exploration of new continents.

The *Renaissance* began in times of religious turmoil. The Middle Ages included a period of political intrigue surrounding the Papacy, culminating in the "Western Schism" in which three men all claimed to be the true Bishop of Rome. "Although the papacy eventually emerged supreme in ecclesiastical matters ... it was dogged by continued accusations of corruption, most famously in the person of Pope Alexander VI who was accused variously of simony, nepotism and fathering four illegitimate children whilst Pope, whom he married off to gain more power." [38]

Shortly thereafter in 1517, Martin Luther published the *95 Thesis* [39] challenging papal authority and criticizing its perceived corruption, particularly in regard to its sale of indulgences -- and the Protestant Reformation began. That became a watershed time in history after the long sleep of the Dark Ages. Europeans were now able to explore new social and religious dimensions. By the 15th century, artists were aware of the transformations that were taking place and were using phrases like *modi antichi* (in the antique manner) or *alle romana lit lalla antica* (in the manner of the Romans and the Ancients). The term *la rinascita* (rebirth) first appeared in 1568.

The *Renaissance* as a cultural movement began in Florence in the 14th century. Various theories have been proposed to account for its origins in Florence, focusing on its social and civic peculiarities; its political structure; the patronage of its dominant family, the Medici; and the migration of Greek scholars to Italy following the Fall of Constantinople at the hands of the Ottoman Turks. [40]

The *Renaissance* is viewed by historians as a bridge between the

Middle Ages and the early Modern Era. The period is best known for its artistic developments and contributions of such men as Michelangelo and Leonardo da Vinci, who inspired the term "*Renaissance man.*"

Does the word, *Renaissance man*, mean anything to you? It was not a word I understood until recently when my son referred to me as such. Since I did not know what it meant -- a compliment or whatever -- I decided to look for a definition, which you can find in the endnote.[41]

This was a remarkable time in the history when men of great vision carried civilization to new heights; Leonardo da Vince was such a person with a remarkable vision for reality. He was a naturalist, an anatomist, an engineer, as well as an artist; was the first modern to realize the true nature of fossils; made note-books of observations that still amaze us; and he was convinced of the possibility of mechanical flight. [42]

Another great name is that of Copernicus, a Pole, who made the first clear analysis of the movements of the heavenly bodies and showed that the earth moves around the sun.

An Italian, Galileo, became the founder of the science of dynamics. Before his time it was believed that a weight a hundred times greater than another would fall a hundred times as fast. Galileo denied this and put it to the test by dropping two unequal weights from the leaning tower of Pisa. He also made the first telescope and developed astronomical views of Copernicus; but the church decided that to believe that the earth was inferior to the sun made Christianity of no account; so Galileo was forced to recant this view and put the earth back in its place as the immovable centre of the universe.

Newton was born in the year after Galileo's death. By his discovery of the law of gravitation, he completed the clear vision of the universe that we have today. [43]

The *Renaissance* particularly highlights the subject of art, so we will look more closely at that in the next chapter.

TEN: RENAISSANCE ART

Great art often follows wealth, which was one of several influences that gave rise to the *Renaissance*. The Medici Bank was important because the trade it generated brought unprecedented wealth to the Italian city, Florence. The pursuit of culture requires financial support and this was provided by Cosimo de' Medici, who set a new standard for the patronage of the arts that was not associated with either the church or monarchy. Then with this financial support other developments followed:

- Oil painting was the most visible development that came with the improvement of oil paints and oil-painting techniques, coupled with a new cadre of artists.
- A "humanist philosophy" that was a secular ideology which espouses reason, ethics, and justice, while specifically rejecting supernatural and religious dogma as a basis of morality and decision making. [44]
- Classical texts, lost to European scholars for centuries, became available. These included Philosophy, Poetry, Drama, Science, and a thesis on the Arts and Early Christian Theology.
- Europe gained access to advanced mathematics, which had its provenance in the works of Islamic scholars.
- The advent of movable type printing, which meant that ideas

in books could be disseminated easily, and an increasing number of books were written for a broad public.

ₒ The serendipitous presence within the region of Florence of a number of individuals of artistic genius, who formed an *ethos* out of which sprang the great masters. [45]

Renaissance art revolved around three towering figures: Leonardo da Vinci, Michelangelo, and Raphael. Each of the three embodied an important aspect of the period: Leonardo was the ultimate *Renaissance man*, a solitary genius to whom no branch of study was foreign; Michelangelo emanated creative power, conceiving vast projects that drew for inspiration on the human body as the ultimate vehicle for emotional expression; Raphael created works that perfectly expressed the classical spirit -- harmonious, beautiful, and serene. [46]

The "universal genius" Leonardo da Vinci perfected aspects of pictorial art: lighting, linear perspective, and anatomy. His adoption of oil paint as his media meant that he could depict light and its effects more naturally and with greater dramatic effect than had ever been done before, as demonstrated in the *Mona Lisa*. His depiction of human emotion in *The Last Supper* set the benchmark for religious painting. Although Leonardo was recognized in his own time as a great artist, his restless researches into anatomy, the nature of flight, and the structure of plant and animal life left him little time to paint. His fame rests on a few completed works; among them are the *Mona Lisa* and the sadly deteriorated fresco *The Last Supper*.

The art of Leonardo's younger contemporary, Michelangelo, took a very different direction with his sculpture and painting. Early sculpture of Michelangelo such as the *Pietà* and the *David* reveals a technical ability with a disposition to bend rules of anatomy and proportion for greater expressive power. Although Michelangelo thought of himself first as a sculptor, his best known work is the giant ceiling fresco of the Sistine Chapel in the Vatican, Rome. It was completed in four years and presents an incredibly complex but philosophically unified composition that fuses traditional Christian theology with Neo-platonic thought. [47]

Standing alongside da Vinci and Michelangelo as the third great

Italian painter of the Renaissance was Raphael, who in a short life span painted a great number of portraits and numerous portrayals of the Madonna and Christ Child, including the *Sistine Madonna.* [48]

While Florence was principle site of the *Renaissance*, a similar heritage of artistic achievement occurred in Venice. It was a major maritime power during the Middle Ages and a staging area for the Crusades as well as an important center of commerce, especially for silk, grain, and spice trade. Its strategic position at the head of the Adriatic Sea made the Venetian naval and commercial power almost invulnerable. The city became a flourishing trade center between Western Europe and the rest of the world, especially the Byzantine Empire and the Islamic world.

Venice is also known for its contributions to the *Renaissance* period. It played an important role in the history of symphonic and operatic music; Mozart, Hayden, and Beethoven all lived there, and Schubert was born there. Venice became one of the most important musical centers of Europe, marked by a characteristic style of composition called the "Venetian school". [49]

The Black Death devastated Venice in 1348 and again in 1575. In those years the plague killed some 50,000 Venetians; then again in 1630, the plague killed a third of Venice's 150.000 citizens. [50]

Venice is famous for its ornate glass art, which it is world-renowned for being colorful and skillfully made. Many of the characteristics of these glass artifacts had been developed by the 13th century. Toward the end of that century, the center of the Venetian glass industry moved to a nearby island, Murano, and the glass produced there is called Murano Glass. In my role as a consultant, I visited Murano with the Technical Director of the Italian glass company, IVIR, who was on the Board of Trustees of the Murano glass museum.

ELEVEN: RENAISSANCE MUSIC

Music development during the *Renaissance* did not enjoy the enormous progress of the other arts such as oil painting and sculpture. It included music that has little meaning for the modern musician: masses, motets, and secular songs such as the frottola, chanson and madrigal. Early precursors of opera such as monody, madrigal comedy, and the intermedio began near the end of the period.

During the *Renaissance* in Florence, instrumental music became a lively salon topic. It was just the thing, some young radicals thought, to be combined with plots based on Greek tragedy for intensifying the emotional impact of the drama. They were soon writing their own songs, which became arias. Many years later, Mozart and his contemporaries began to write orchestral accompaniment to their recitations. These young Florentines in effect became the first opera composers. [51]

It was at this time that a technical innovation, the *basso continuo*, [52] was developed that made Italian opera possible. This was a kind of musical shorthand invented for the benefit of the keyboard musician who had to fill in the harmonics left bare by orchestra and soloist. The use of the *basso continuo* freed melodic parts and the result of this freedom was the establishment of the solo virtuoso. He soon took the spotlight from the composer and to this day represents musical glamour to the public. [53]

With vocal virtuosity as a model, it was no great step for Italian composers to start writing purely instrumental music and it was to the violin, the most sensitively expressive of all instruments, to which they turned. The violin movement was centered in the town of Cremona where the Stradivari, Guarneri, and Amati families were turning out hundreds of matchless instruments. Experts are still trying to determine the secrets that made those violins so resonant, so sweet, or even-voiced across the entire range. [54]

As instrumental musical compositions grew longer, they tended to become monotonous for the listener. This led to the development of two musical forms that later became the foundation for much of modern music. The first was the *binary* form, which repeated itself from beginning to end with a concluding flourish to make it sound more finished the second time around. This binary form was used by Scarlatti and J.S. Bach. Opera composers developed a three-part *Ternary* form, which is diagramed by the letters "A-B-A". This is the foundation of a vast body of music: most of the first, second, and third movements of symphonies, sonatas, string quartets, and today's popular songs. [55]

The Italians' facile melodies became the rage of Europe -- and the despair of serious composers in other countries. The north European composers began to curtail virtuoso display for display's sake and substituted more detailed writing. As they did so, they found that some of the frills and arabesques of the virtuoso style were useful for more serious purposes as well. A trill, for instance, when spun out at the proper moment, could produce a feeling of tense expectancy; the up-down-up convolutions of a turn, when wrapped slowly around its fundamental note, could result in a languorous effect; a rapid scale passage could be made to indicate anger or ecstasy or a storm at sea. Other decorative devices, such as delaying a harmonic point of rest, proved to be emotionally disturbing. [56]

At this point, the fundamentals of music were all present.

TWELVE: BAROQUE PERIOD

The *Baroque* era followed the *Renaissance* and roughly coincides with the 17th century. The word that distinguishes the *Baroque* period is style: the desire to evoke emotion by appealing to the senses. Some of the qualities frequently associated with *Baroque* are grandeur, sensuous richness, drama, vitality, movement, tension, and emotional exuberance.

The term *Baroque* probably derived from the Italian word "barocco", which was used by philosophers to describe an obstacle in logic. Subsequently the word came to denote any contorted idea or involuted process of thought. Another possible source is the Portuguese word "barroco", used to describe an irregular or imperfectly shaped pearl, and this usage still survives in the jeweler's term "baroque pearl". The word came to be used to describe anything irregular, bizarre, or otherwise departing from established rules and proportions. This biased view of 17th-century art styles was held until the 19th century and the term always carried the implication of odd, grotesque, exaggerated, and over-decorated. [57]

This was a time of religious turmoil during the 30 year war between Catholics and Protestants that ended in 1648 with the Peace of Westphalia, helping establish Protestantism in Northern Europe; and the *Baroque* period was somewhat the outgrowth of that conflict. The popularity of the *Baroque* style was encouraged by the Roman Catholic Church, which had decided at the time of the Council of

Trent in response to the Protestant Reformation that the arts should communicate religious themes with emotional involvement; and the church was urging that paintings and sculptures should speak to the illiterate rather than to the well-informed. [58] In our modern vernacular, this was an attempt by the Church to develop a PR (public relations) program to become more relevant to the times. The Jesuits adopted *Baroque* for their churches and were instrumental in spreading it throughout most of Europe. [59]

The aristocracy saw the dramatic style of *Baroque* art and architecture as a means of impressing visitors and expressing triumphant power and control. Palaces were built with an elegant entrance to the court, grand staircase, and reception room of sequentially increasing opulence. The word *Baroque* can simply mean that something is "elaborate" with many details. [60]

This was the time when exploration and settlements in the Americas' began with the Jamestown colony in Virginia in 1607 and the Plymouth colony in Massachusetts in 1620. Harvard University was chartered in 1636 outside Boston. This was also the time when Shakespeare lived. "He is the greatest writer in the English language and the world's pre-eminent dramatist, producing 38 plays, 154 sonnets, and two long narrative poems. He produced most of his best known works between 1589 and 1613. While he wrote and his plays were performed during the *Baroque* era, his reputation did not rise to his present heights until later during the *Romantic* period." [61]

Baroque architecture originated in Italy in the early 17th century, and was prevalent in Europe and the New World for a century and a half. "It is characterized by use of the Greek classical orders in columns, dynamic opposition, and the dramatic combined effects of architecture, sculpture, painting, and the decorative arts. ... New emphasis was placed on bold massing, colonnades, domes, light-and-shade color effects, and the bold play of volume and void. ... The other *Baroque* innovation was the state apartment, a sequence of increasingly rich interiors that culminated in a chamber or throne room or a state bedroom. The sequence of monumental stairs followed by a state apartment was copied in smaller scale in aristocratic dwellings." [62]

Baroque architecture was taken up with enthusiasm in Germany. In England it was embodied in work by their premier architect, Sir Christopher Wren. He rebuilt 51 churches after the Great Fire of London, including St Paul's Cathedral. Many examples of *Baroque* architecture and town planning are found in other European towns and in Latin America. An example is the Cathedral of Morelia Michoacán in Mexico. Built in the 17th century, it is one of many *Baroque* cathedrals in the Americas.

Baroque theatre had elaborate multiplicity of plot turns and variety of situations characteristic of Shakespeare's tragedies. Theatre became a multimedia experience. Much of the technology used in current Broadway plays was developed during this era. The stage could change from a romantic garden to the interior of a palace in a matter of seconds. The entire stage became a framed area that allowed the audience to see only a specific action, hiding all the machinery and technology -- mostly ropes and pulleys. [63]

Many forms of music were born during the era like the opera, concerto, and sinfonia. The application of the term "*Baroque*" to music is a recent development; the first use of the word was only in 1919, and it was not until 1940 that it was first used in English. The term was initially used with a derogatory meaning to underline the excesses in emphasis, eccentric redundancy, and noisy abundance of details; which contrasted with the rationality of the *Renaissance*. In reviewing an opera, "a critic described it as *baroque*, complaining that the music lacked coherent melody, was filled with unremitting dissonances, constantly changed key and meter, and speedily ran through every compositional device." [64]

Baroque still forms a portion of the music repertoire being performed and listened to today. Composers of the era include Bach, Handel, and Vivaldi.

Johann Sebastian Bach was born in Germany in 1685 in a family of church organists. He was a composer, organists, harpsichordist, and violist; whose works brought the era it to its ultimate maturity. [65] "His was a world where composing was respected and as earthly a craft as carpentry. ... Young Sebastian, who became a competent fiddler almost as soon as he could draw a bow, learned to help out in the town orchestra as today's teen-ager might help out with the family dishes. ... By the time he was 15, he was an accomplished musician with a pretty singing voice, a good fiddle technique, and a better one on the organ." [66]

Bach's works include: *The Well-tempered Clavier*, *Mass in B Minor*, *Magnificant*, *The Art of Fugue*, sonatas for violin, the Cello suites, more than 200 surviving cantatas, and a similar number of organ works. He was not widely recognized until a revival of his music in the 19th century, but is now regarded as one of the great composers of all time. [67] (Have you ever listened to Bach? I think his music is tedious and boring!)

George Frideric Handel was a German-British composer, famous for his operas, oratorios, and concertos. Handel was born in Germany. He received musical training in Italy before settling in London and becoming a naturalized British subject. His works include *Messiah*, *Water Music*, and *Music for the Royal Fireworks*. Handel was a transitional composer whose music became well-known to those of the next *Classical* period, such as Haydn, Mozart, and Beethoven. We will look at them in the next chapter.

THIRTEEN: CLASSICAL PERIOD OF MUSIC

There are two different uses for the word "classical". The term often refers to a variety of styles when people say, "I love to listen to classical music." That may include music from a variety of eras such as Mozart, Tchaikovsky, and Bernstein. A different use for the term is more specific and refers to music of the *Classical* period between the years 1750 to 1830. This chapter is about the latter.

The *Classical* period followed the *Baroque* Period. The best known composers are Joseph Haydn, Wolfgang Amadeus Mozart, Ludwig van Beethoven, and Franz Schubert. This time is sometimes referred to as the era of *Viennese Classic*, since Mozart, Haydn, and Beethoven all worked at some time in Vienna and Schubert was born there. [68]

The great music created by these men occurred during a turbulent time in Europe and America:

- o 1755-1763 Britain and France fought over India and control of the Americas.
- o 1776 United States declares its independence.
- o 1789 Storming of the Bastille, the French Revolution begins, and Louis XVI loses his head on the guillotine.
- o 1797 Napoleon begins his rise, and in 1804 becomes emperor.
- o 1815 Battle of Waterloo and end of Napoleon's reign.
- o 1834 Beginning of the reign of Queen Victoria.

Amidst all the turmoil, the creation of great music and architecture continued to develop. In the middle of the 18th century, Europe began to move toward a new style in architecture and the arts, generally known as "Classicism", which sought to emulate the ideals of classical antiquity and especially those of Greece. While still tightly linked to the court culture, the new style favored contrasts and simplicity rather than complexity. The development of "natural philosophy" had established itself in the public consciousness: Newton's physics was taken as a paradigm, and axioms were well-articulated and orderly. [69]

Structural clarity worked its way into the world of music, moving away from the polyphony (many tones or voices) to a style where a melody over a subordinate harmony -- a combination called homophony -- was preferred. The playing of chords became a more prevalent feature of music.

The new *Classic* style was also affected by changes in the social structure. As the 18th century progressed, the nobility became the primary patrons of instrumental music. Changes in the economic situation also had the effect of improving the quality of musicians. The concerto and sonata became more defined, and the symphony was created in this period (this is attributed to Joseph Haydn). The "concerto grosso" (a concerto for more than one musician) began to be replaced by the "solo concerto" (a concerto featuring only one soloist), and placed importance on the soloist's ability to show-off. Some concerto grossos remained, the most famous being Mozart's *Sinfonia Concertante for Violin and Viola in E flat Major.*

Classical period music has a lighter texture than *Baroque* and is less complex. Contrast within melodies, changes of mood, and timbre were more commonplace. Melodies tended to be shorter with clear-cut phrases and clearly marked cadences. The orchestra increased in size and range. As a solo instrument, the harpsichord was replaced by the piano. Importance was given to instrumental music: string quartet, symphony, concerto, and sonata form. By the late 1750's there were flourishing centers of the new style in Italy, Vienna, and Paris and dozens of symphonies had been composed. [70]

The first great master of the style was the composer Joseph Haydn.

He composed over forty symphonies in the 1760's alone. He was later overshadowed by Mozart and Beethoven, but before their pre-eminence, Haydn had reached a place in music above other composers except perhaps for Handel from the *Baroque* era. He took existing ideas, and radically altered how they functioned -- earning Haydn the title "Father of the Symphony. [71]

Haydn's younger contemporary, Wolfgang Amadeus Mozart, brought his genius to Haydn's ideas and applied them to two of the major genres of the day: opera, and the virtuoso concerto. He rapidly came to the attention of Haydn, who hailed the new composer, studied his works, and considered the younger man his only true peer in music. You can read about Mozart in the next chapter. Ludwig van Beethoven followed Mozart and was an admirer. You can read about him in a later chapter.

When Haydn and Mozart began composing, symphonies were played as single movements within other works -- and many of them lasted only ten or twelve minutes; instrumental groups had varying standards of playing; and the continuo was a central part of music. In the intervening years, music had seen dramatic changes:

- o international touring had grown explosively,
- o concert societies were beginning to be formed,
- o musical notations had been made more specific and descriptive, and schematics for works had been simplified. [72]

It was time for a change. A transition to the *Romantic* Period had already started.

FOURTEEN: WOLFGANG AMADEUS MOZART

If you failed to see the Hollywood movie, *Amadeus*, (1984) you missed one of the best movies of all times. The film received eight academy awards, including Best Picture. More than just a portrait of Mozart, it was a compelling picture that focused on the social environment and historical times of the *Classical* Period.

Wolfgang Amadeus Mozart composed over 600 works, many acknowledged as pinnacles of symphonic, concerto, piano, operatic, and choral music. He is among the most popular of classical composers. [73] Mozart showed prodigious ability from his earliest childhood in Salzburg. Already competent on keyboard and violin, he composed from the age of five and performed before European royalty. At age 17, he became a court musician in Salzburg, but grew restless and travelled in search of a better position (and more salary), always composing abundantly. While visiting Vienna, he was dismissed from his Salzburg position and chose to stay in Vienna, where he achieved fame but little financial security. During his years in Vienna, he composed many of his best-known symphonies, concertos, and operas, and portions of the Requiem, which was largely unfinished at the time of his death. He was survived by his wife Constanze and two sons.

Mozart was born to Leopold and Anna Maria Mozart in Salzburg, capital of the sovereign Archbishopric of Salzburg in Austria, at the time part of the Holy Roman Empire. His only sibling to survive infancy was his elder sister Maria Anna, nicknamed "Nannerl". His father Leopold was deputy Kapellmeister to the court orchestra of the Archbishop of Salzburg, and a minor composer. When Mozart was age 4, his father began to teach him minuets and pieces at the clavier. At the age of five, he was already composing little pieces, which he played to his father who wrote them down. Leopold eventually gave up composing when his son's musical talents became evident.

During Mozart's youth, his family made several European journeys in which he and Nannerl performed as child prodigies. A long concert tour spanning three and a half years followed. During this trip, Mozart met a great number of musicians and acquainted himself with the works of other composers. A particularly important influence was Johann Christian Bach, whom Mozart visited in London. These trips were often arduous. Travel conditions were primitive; the family had to wait for invitations and reimbursement from the nobility. They endured long, near-fatal illnesses far from home: first Leopold was ill and then both children.

Mozart was employed as a court musician by the ruler of Salzburg, Prince-Archbishop Colloredo. (This was the locale and setting of the movie *Amadeus*.) The composer had a great number of friends and admirers in Salzburg and had the opportunity to work in many genres, composing symphonies, sonatas, string quartets, serenades, and a few operas. He developed an enthusiasm for violin concertos, producing a series of five. In 1776 he turned his efforts to piano concertos. Despite these artistic successes, Mozart grew increasingly discontented with Salzburg and redoubled his efforts to find a position elsewhere. One reason was his low salary. Mozart also longed to compose operas, and Salzburg provided only rare occasions for these.

Mozart resigned his Salzburg position and ventured out in search of employment. In Germany he fell in love with Aloysia Weber, one of four daughters in a musical family. Sometime later, he again encountered Aloysia, now a very successful singer, but she made it plain she was no longer interested in him; however, Mozart moved in with the Weber family that needed his resources. The father had died, and they were now taking in lodgers to make ends meet. Aloysia, who had rejected

Mozart's suit, was now married, and Mozart's interest shifted to the third daughter, Constanze. Even though the courtship did not go smoothly, they were finally married and had six children, of which only two survived infancy.

With substantial returns from his concerts and elsewhere, he and Constanze adopted a rather plush lifestyle. They moved to an expensive apartment, and Mozart bought an elegant fortepiano and a fine billiard table -- all beyond their means. The Mozart's sent their son to an expensive boarding school, and kept servants. Saving was therefore impossible, and the short period of financial success did nothing to soften the hardship the Mozart's were later to experience.

1786 saw the successful premiere of The Marriage of Figaro in Vienna, and its reception in Prague was even warmer. The opera Don Giovanni premiered in 1787 to acclaim in Prague, and also met with success in Vienna. The two are among Mozart's most important works and are mainstays of the operatic repertoire today.

Around 1786, he had ceased to appear frequently in public concerts, and his income shrank. This was a difficult time for musicians in Vienna because Austria was at war, and the level of prosperity and the ability of the aristocracy to support music had declined.

Mozart's last year was a time of great productivity. He composed some of his most admired works: the opera The Magic Flute, the final piano concerto, the Clarinet Concerto , the last in his series of string quintets, Ave Verum Corpus , and the unfinished Requiem.

Mozart fell ill while in Prague for the premiere of his opera La clemenza di Tito, written for the Emperor's coronation festivities. The illness intensified at which point Mozart became bedridden, suffering from swelling, pain, and vomiting. Mozart was nursed in his final illness by Constanze, and died in December 1791 at the age of 35. (Death at age of only 35!! Imagine what he had accomplished musically in that short life time). The cause of death cannot be known with certainty. Researchers have hinted at many causes of death, including trichinosis, influenza, mercury poisoning, and a rare kidney ailment. The most widely accepted hypothesis is that Mozart died of acute rheumatic fever.

Mozart was buried in a common grave, in accordance with contemporary Viennese custom, at a cemetery outside the city. No mourners attended, which was consistent with Viennese burial customs at the time. He was raised a Roman Catholic and remained a member of the Church throughout his life. He enjoyed billiards and dancing, and kept pets: a canary, a starling, a dog, and also a horse for recreational riding.

As portrayed in the movie, Mozart was both a musical genius and also a very ordinary human being.

FIFTEEN: BEETHOVEN

Ludwig van Beethoven was a German composer, and a crucial figure in the transition between the Classical and Romantic eras. He remains one of the most famous and influential composers of all time.

Born in Bonn in 1770, Beethoven moved to Vienna in his early twenties, studying with Joseph Haydn and quickly gaining a reputation as a virtuoso pianist. His hearing began to deteriorate ten years later in the late 1790's, yet he continued to compose, conduct, and perform, even after becoming completely deaf. Beethoven's first music teacher was his father. While his musical talent manifested itself early and he was performing by age eight, he did not have the mercurial rise in fame as the young Mozart. Beethoven began working as an assistant organist at age eleven.

At the age of eighteen, Beethoven traveled to Vienna apparently in the hope of studying with Mozart, but he learned that his mother was severely ill, and returned home. His mother died shortly thereafter, and the father lapsed into alcoholism. As a result, Beethoven became responsible for the care of his two younger brothers, and he spent the next five years in Bonn.

Beethoven left Bonn again for Vienna in 1792, amid rumors of war spilling out of France. The French Revolution had started a couple years earlier and all of Europe was in turmoil. In Vienna, Beethoven responded to the widespread feeling that he was a successor to the recently deceased Mozart by studying that master's work and writing works with a distinctly Mozartean flavor. Working under Haydn's direction, he sought to master counterpoint and also studied violin. By 1793, he had established a reputation in Vienna as a piano virtuoso. Beethoven then tackled composition with a string quartet and the symphony. With the composition of his first six string quartets and premieres of the First and Second Symphonies, Beethoven became one of the most important composers following Haydn and Mozart.

Beethoven taught piano to the daughters of a Hungarian Countess, and while the lessons lasted less than one month, he formed a relationship with the older daughter Josephine, but shortly after these lessons, she married a German Count. Beethoven became a regular visitor at their house, teaching, and playing at parties. While her marriage was unhappy, her relationship with Beethoven did not intensify until after her husband died.

Around 1796 at the age of 26, Beethoven began to lose his hearing. He suffered a severe form of tinnitus, a "ringing" in his ears that made it hard for him to perceive music; he also avoided conversation. The cause of Beethoven's deafness is unknown. On the advice of his doctor, he lived in a small Austrian town just outside Vienna in an attempt to come to terms with his condition. There he wrote a letter to his brothers that records his thoughts of suicide due to his growing deafness, and records his resolution to continue living for his art. The hearing loss did not prevent his composing music, but it made playing at concerts -- a lucrative source of income -- increasingly difficult. After a failed attempt to perform his own works, he never performed in public again.

A particular trauma for Beethoven occurred during this period in 1809, when the attacking forces of Napoleon bombarded Vienna. Beethoven, very worried that the noise would destroy what remained of his hearing, hid in the basement of his brother's house, covering his ears with pillows. He was composing the Emperor Concerto at the time.

That Beethoven knew what he was writing into his masterpieces is beyond question. He did his preliminary work in sketchbooks, many of which have been saved. They show his compositions came to him first as basic structures with all the fundamental harmonies and counterpoint complete -- often before he had even thought of the tunes. The tunes themselves, even the most ingenuous, are the products of a vast amount of honing and polishing. The lovely melody of the fifth symphony's slow movement is a case in point. When it first occurred to Beethoven, it was a trite, bouncy little thing. As he put it through version after version, it became more refined. "Simplify! Simplify!" he wrote in the margin of his notebook. [74]

Beethoven had a number of romances and proposed marriage to several women, but all turned him down and married someone else.

He met Giulietta Guicciardi in 1800 and dedicated to her Sonata No. 14, popularly known as the Moonlight Sonata (which I played on the piano -- but not very well -- when I was in high school). Marriage plans were thwarted by Giulietta's father. In 1803 she married Count Wenzel Robert von Gallenberg.

Beethoven's relationship with Josephine Deym deepened after the death of her husband. He proposed to her but she turned him down, and their relationship ended. She cited her "duty", a reference that she was born of nobility and he was a commoner.

He also proposed to Therese Malfatti in 1810; his common status may also have interfered with those plans. He began a relationship in 1804 with a married woman, Josephine Brunsvik. Some of his (married) romantic partners had children (leading to assertions of Beethoven's possible paternity).

Beethoven was finally motivated to begin significant composition again in June 1813, when news arrived of the defeat of one of Napoleon's armies in Spain by a coalition of forces under the Duke of Wellington. This news stimulated him to write the battle symphony known as Wellington's Victory.

Beethoven had a turbulent private life. It is thought in hindsight that he suffered with what is now called a bipolar condition. After subjecting himself to a fruitless bout with his ear doctors, he gave up conducting and went into seclusion. He quarreled with his servants, convinced that they cheated him; double-crossed his publishers and patrons (he sold several compositions twice, including the ninth symphony); maligned the Viennese when they took a fancy to the operas of Rossini; and was even suspicious of his royalty friends when they suspended his allowance temporarily because of currency collapse. [75]

Beethoven's output dropped, which he attributed to an "inflammatory fever" that afflicted him for more than a year. He was bedridden for most of his remaining life and died on 26 March 1827, at the age of 57, during a thunderstorm. A friend who was present at the time claimed that there was a peal of thunder at the moment of death. An autopsy revealed significant liver damage, which may have been due to heavy alcohol consumption.

Beethoven's funeral procession on 29 March 1827 was attended by an estimated 20,000 Viennese citizens. Franz Schubert, who died the following year and was buried next to Beethoven, was one of the torchbearers. Unlike Mozart, who was buried anonymously in a communal grave (the custom at the time), Beethoven was buried in a dedicated grave after a requiem mass at the church of the Holy Trinity.

Beethoven is acknowledged as one of the giants of music. He was also a pivotal figure in the transition from the 18th century *Classical* period to the 19th century *Romanitic* period, and his influence on subsequent generations of composers was profound.

SIXTEEN: ROMANTIC PERIOD OF MUSIC

This moment in history was again ripe for dramatic shift, and the culture of the *Classic* period was followed by the *Romantic* period. Romanticism was a rejection of the order, calm, harmony, balance, and rationality that typified Classicism. It emphasized the emotional, irrational, imaginative, and spontaneous, feelings of music. [76]

This evolution in cultures became the basis for the music from the second decade of the 19th century to the early 20th century. It was characterized by increased attention to a melody as well as expressive and emotional elements, which paralleled romanticism in other art forms. Music began to break from the *Classical* period with pieces like nocturnes, fantasias, and preludes being written in which development of themes were minimized. The music became more chromatic, dissonant, and tonally colorful. [77]

These changes in musical tastes paralleled those in society in general. Musical institutions emerged from the control of wealthy patrons and musicians could construct lives independent of the nobility. Increasing interest in music by the growing middle classes spurred organizations for the teaching and performance of music. The piano became widely popular. Many symphony orchestras date their founding to this period, and the size of the orchestra (typically around 40 in the *Classical* period) grew to be over 100. European music culture found new root in America. There was also a rise of nationalism in music (echoing political sentiments of the time), as composers such as Edward Grieg, Nikolai Rimsky-Korsakov, and Antonin Dvorak reflected traditional music of their homelands in their compositions. [78]

A new generation of composers emerged. The most significant of these was Ludwig van Beethoven, a transitional composer from the *Classical* period (who we discussed in the last chapter). He is claimed by romantics as one of their number because they thought he had abandoned the strict forms of classicism. Much of the vitality and richness of his music lies in his use of thematic "development". This process has become so much a part of the musical scheme of things that it is practically a requirement for great music." [79]

The *Romantic* period occurred during the era when Napoleon was rising to power, and wars and politics intervened in the lives of many musicians, including Beethoven. He was much taken with Napoleon Bonaparte and initially dedicated his *Eroica Symphony* to him. Then in hearing that Napoleon had made himself emperor, Beethoven erased the dedication and replaced it with the words, "*to the memory of a great man,*" as if the hero was already dead. The first movement of the *Eroica Symphony* is of superhuman proportions -- It quite literally frightened its early listeners. It begins with two crashing chords. [80]

Other composers of the *Romantic* Period include Schubert, Franz Liszt, Antonio Vivaldi, Handel, Frederic Chopin, Richard Wagner, Giuseppe Verdi, Johann Strauss, Johannes Brahms, Niccolo Paganini, Georges Bizet, Antonio Dvorak, Pyotr Ilyich Tchaikovsky, and Giccomo Puccini.

My two favorites are the Russian, Pyotr Ilyich Tchaikovsky, and the Italian opera composer, Giccomo Puccini. Tchaikovsky's output includes symphonies, operas, ballets, instrumentals, chamber music, and songs. He wrote some of the most popular concert and theatrical music in the *Romantic* repertoire, including the *1812 Overture*, his *First Piano concerto*, the last three of his numbered symphonies, the opera *Eugene Onegin*, and the ballets *Swan Lake, Sleeping Beauty,* and the *Nutcracker*. You can read more about his life in the following chapter. Giccomo Puccini composed two of my favorite operas: *Madame Butterfly* and *La boheme*. He is discussed in a later chapter.

SEVENTEEN: PYOTR ILYICH TCHAIKOVSKY

Пётр Ильич Чайковский

My favorite composer of the *Romantic* period is Pyotr Ilyich Tchaikovsky. He was born in Russia in 1840, the son of a French immigrant. Tchaikovsky began piano lessons at the age of five. A precocious pupil, he could read music as adeptly as his teacher within three years. His early musical studies were in the St. Petersburg Conservatory where his master was the famed pianist Anton Rubinstein. When he was 26, he got a position at a conservatory in Moscow. His first success was the opera, *The Voyevoda*, taking no less than 15 personal curtain calls. [81]

At the age of 28, Tchaikovsky met the Belgian soprano Desiree Artot, then on a tour of Russia. They became infatuated and were engaged to be married. He dedicated his *Romance in F minor for piano* to her. However, without any communication with Tchaikovsky, Artot married a member of her company, a Spanish baritone. Tchaikovsky later claimed she was the only woman he ever loved.

Tchaikovsky's ill-starred marriage to one of his former composition students, Antonina Miliukova, soon followed. The brief time with his new wife drove him to an emotional crisis, which was followed by a stay in Switzerland for rest and recovery. They remained legally married but never lived together again nor had any children, though she later gave birth to three children by another man. Tchaikovsky's marital debacle may have forced him to face the full truth concerning his homosexuality. He wrote to his brother:

> *"Thanks to the regularity of my life, to the sometimes tedious but always inviolable calm, and above all, thanks to time which heals all wounds, I have completely recovered from my insanity. There's no doubt that for some months on end I was a bit insane, and only now, when I'm completely recovered, have I learned to relate objectively to everything which I did during my brief insanity. That man who in May took it into his head to marry Antonina Ivanova, who during June wrote a whole opera as though nothing had happened, who in July married, who in September fled from his wife, who in November railed at Rome and so on—that man wasn't I, but another Pyotr Ilyich."*

A few days later, he added that there was:

> *"nothing more futile than wanting to be anything other than what I am by nature."* [82]

The strain of the marriage and Tchaikovsky's emotional state may have enhanced Tchaikovsky's creativity. The *Fourth Symphony* and the opera Eugene Onegin, two of his finest compositions, are held up as proof of this enhanced creativity. He finished both these works in the six months between his engagement and the completion of the rest cure following his marriage breakdown. The intensity of personal emotion now flowing through Tchaikovsky's works was entirely new to Russian music. It prompted some Russian commentators to place his name alongside that of novelist Dostoyevsky. A critic wrote of Tchaikovsky and Dostoyevsky:

> *"With a hidden passion they both stop at moments of horror, total spiritual collapse, and finding acute sweetness in the cold trepidation of the heart before the abyss, they both force the reader to experience those feelings, too."* [83]

Tchaikovsky began to shed his unsociability and restlessness. Tsar Alexander III conferred upon him the Order of St. Vladimir, which carried with it hereditary nobility and won Tchaikovsky a personal audience with the Tsar. The Tsar's decoration was a visible seal of official approval that helped Tchaikovsky's social rehabilitation. This came with the extreme success of his Orchestral Suite No. 3. After its premiere in Saint Petersburg, Tchaikovsky wrote:

"I have never seen such a triumph. I saw the whole audience was moved, and grateful to me. These moments are the finest adornments of an artist's life. Thanks to these it is worth living and laboring." [84]

In 1869 at the age of 29, Tchaikovsky composed his first masterpiece, the fantasy-overture Romeo and Juliet. Some of his best-known works from this early period include the First Piano Concerto, Variations on a Rococo Theme for cello and orchestra, the Little Russian and Fourth Symphonies, the ballet Swan Lake and the opera Eugene Onegin.

Tchaikovsky's fame among concert audiences began to expand. While his reputation grew, a corresponding increase in performances of his works did not occur until he began conducting them himself, starting in the mid-1880s. All of the operas Tchaikovsky had completed up to that point had been staged, and his orchestral works had been given performances that had been well received. He was honored by the Tsar, and lauded in the concert halls of the world. [85]

Tchaikovsky was an avid letter-writer and corresponded with many. This from a letter he wrote to a friend in 1878:

"Yesterday I received your letter with the news of Rubenstein's concert. I am so glad you are pleased with my concerto. ... Why do you not care for Mozart? In this respect our opinions differ, my good friend. I not only like Mozart, I idolize him. To me the most beautiful opera ever written is Don Juan. It is true Mozart used up his forces too generously and often wrote without inspiration, because he was compelled by want. Even Bach and Beethoven have

> *left a considerable number of inferior works which are not worthy*
> *to be spoken of in the same breath as their masterpieces."* [86]

In 1885, after Tchaikovsky resettled in Russia, the Tsar asked personally for a new production of Eugene Onegin to be staged in Saint Petersburg. News of the opera's success spread, and the work was produced by opera houses throughout Russia and abroad. Tchaikovsky was awarded a lifetime pension from the Tsar. This essentially made him the premier court composer.

Conducting brought him to America in 1891, where he led the New York Music Society's orchestra in his *Festival Coronation March* at the inaugural concert of New York's Carnegie Hall. In 1888 Tchaikovsky led the premiere of his Fifth Symphony in Saint Petersburg. While the work was received with extreme enthusiasm by audiences, critics proved hostile, calling the symphony "routine" and "meretricious." (Of course, I personally know the critics were grossly wrong, because the *Fifth Symphony* is one of my favorite symphonic pieces. See Appendix G for an excerpt from my previous book, *SONGS AND RECIPES:For Macho Men Only.*)

Tchaikovsky wrote many works which are popular with the classical music public, including his Romeo and Juliet, the 1812 Overture, his three ballets (The Nutcracker, Swan Lake, The Sleeping Beauty) and Marche Slave. These, along with two of his four concertos, three of his six numbered symphonies and, of his 10 operas, The Queen of Spades and Eugene Onegin, are among his most familiar works. Almost as popular are the Manfred Symphony, Francesca da Rimini, the Capriccio Italien and the Serenade for Strings. His three string quartets and piano trio all contain beautiful passages, while recitalists still perform some of his 106 songs. Tchaikovsky also wrote over a hundred piano works, covering the entire span of his creative life.

Tchaikovsky died in Saint Petersburg on November 6, 1893, nine days after the premiere of his Sixth Symphony, the *Pathétique.* Though only 53 years old, he lived a long life compared to many Russian composers. He was interred near the graves of fellow-composers Borodin, Glinka, and Mussorgsky, Rimsky-Korsakov and Balakirev.

Tchaikovsky's death has traditionally been attributed to cholera, most probably contracted through drinking contaminated water several days earlier.

He is considered a transitional composer, because his music is in today's repertoire as part of our modern musical era.

EIGHTEEN: GICCOMO PUCCINI

Giacomo Antonio Domenico Michele Secondo Maria Puccini

Puccini was an Italian composer whose operas, including La bohème, Tosca, Madama Butterfly, and Turandot, are among the most frequently performed in the American repertoire. While considered from the *Romantic* period of music, he could be considered transitional into the Modern era because he premiered one of his operas in New York City in 1918; and some of his arias, such as *Che gelida manina* from *La bohème,* have become part of American popular culture. This solo, *My name is Mimi*, of all operatic arias is a favorite of mine.

Puccini was born in Lucca in Tuscany, into a family with five generations of musical history behind them. His father died when Giacomo was five years old, and he was sent to study with his uncle. It was not until he saw a performance of Verdi's Aida that he became inspired to be an opera composer. He and his brother walked 18 miles to see the performance in Pisa. In 1880 at the age of 21, Puccini enrolled in the Milan Conservatory. In the same year he composed the *Messa*, the culmination of his family's long association with church music; it refers to a prayer of the Roman Catholic Mass. "The work anticipated Puccini's career as an operatic composer with glimpses of the dramatic power he would bring forth; the powerful arias are more operatic than is usual in church music and the *Messa* compares interestingly with Verdi's Requiem." [87]

While studying at the Conservatory, Puccini entered a competition for a one-act opera; he lost the competition and blamed the loss on the librettist. In his next operatic attempt, four other librettists were involved due to Puccini constantly changing his mind about the structure of the piece. The final two, Illica and Giacosa, came together to complete the opera, and remained with Puccini for his next three operas and probably his greatest successes: *La boheme, Tosca* and *Madama Butterfly.* [88]

In a scandalous episode for Italy, Puccini eloped with a married woman, Elvira Gemignani. He was able to survive the scandal because his next opera was successful, and Puccini went on to become the leading operatic composer of his day.

From 1891 onwards, Puccini spent most of his time at Torre del Lago, a small community about fifteen miles from Lucca situated between the Ligurian Sea and Lake Massaciuccoli. He built a villa on the lake, now known as the "Villa Museo Puccini." After his death, a mausoleum was created and the composer is buried there in the chapel, along with his wife and son who died later. The Villa Museo Puccini is presently owned by his granddaughter and is open to the public. [89]

After 1904, compositions were less frequent. Following his passion for driving fast cars, Puccini was nearly killed in a major accident. In 1909, there was scandal after Puccini's wife, Elvira, falsely accused their maid of having an affair with Puccini. The maid then committed suicide. Elvira was successfully sued and Giacomo had to pay damages. A habitual cigar and cigarette chain smoker, Puccini began to complain of chronic sore throats. A diagnosis of throat cancer led his doctors to recommend a new radiation therapy treatment, which was being offered in Brussels. Puccini died there in 1924, at the age of 65, from complications after the treatment. News of his death reached Rome during a performance of *La bohème.* The opera was immediately stopped, and the orchestra played Chopin's Funeral March for the stunned audience.

Turandot, his final opera, was left unfinished, and the last two scenes were completed by Franco Alfano based on the composer's sketches. When Arturo Toscanini conducted the premiere performance in front of a sold-out crowd, with every prominent Italian except for Benito Mussolini in attendance, he chose not to perform Alfano's portion of the score. The performance reached the point where Puccini had completed the score, at which time Toscanini stopped the orchestra. The conductor turned to the audience and said: "Here the opera finishes, because at this point the Maestro died." At which time the opera closed to thunderous applause. [90]

Unlike Verdi and Wagner, Puccini did not appear to be active in the politics of his day. However, Mussolini, Fascist dictator of Italy at the time, claimed that Puccini applied for admission to the National Fascist Party. Puccini was among the early supporters of the Fascist party, but there are no records indicating he was ever an active member. This notwithstanding, Fascist propaganda appropriated Puccini's figure, and one of the most widely played marches during Fascist street parades and public ceremonies was the *"Inno a Roma"* (Hymn to Rome), composed in 1919.

The structures of Puccini's works are noteworthy. While it is possible to divide his operas into arias, his scores present a sense of continuous flow and connectivity. Puccini used leitmotifs [91] to connote characters and sentiments. This is apparent in *Tosca*, where the three chords which signal the beginning of the opera are used throughout to announce Scarpia. Several motifs are also linked to Mimi and the bohemians in *La bohème* and to Cio-Cio-San's eventual suicide in *Butterfly*. Another distinctive quality in Puccini's works is the use of the voice in the style of speech i.e. *canto parlando* -- characters sing short phrases one after another as if they were in conversation. Puccini is also celebrated for his melodic gift and many of his melodies are enduringly popular. Unusual for operas written by Italian composers until that time, many of Puccini's operas are set outside Italy -- in exotic places such as Japan (*Madama Butterfly*), gold-mining country in California (*La fanciulla del West*), Paris and the Riviera (*La rondine*), and China (*Turandot*).

NINETEEN: MODERN MUSIC

Now we come to modern music. Like many other things, it carries legacies from the past. Our American music came from two sources: European music such as symphonic, opera, or ballet; and music that originated in slave communities of the American South that grew into the new genre of *jazz*.

European music remains as a major part of our modern repertoire. This came from composers of the *Romantic* period such as Tchaikovsky and Puccini who were a bridge into the 20th century. Tchaikovsky conducted the New York Music Society orchestra at the inaugural concert in Carnegie Hall. Puccini premiered an opera in New York City in 1918.

Concurrently with the import of European classics, a musical birth took place in the American South with Black slaves who had brought their musical heritage with them from Africa. It found its expression in their new environment with "work songs" and "field hollars". This music made its way into the saloons and bordellos of New Orleans, eventually reaching a unique expression in a new genre called *jazz*. An early proponent was Louis Armstrong who joined the Fletcher Henderson dance band in 1924 as featured soloist. That same year, Paul Whiteman commissioned George Gershwin's *Rhapsody in Blue*, a sophisticated composition of *jazz*; and Duke Ellington opened at New York City's Cotton Club in 1927.

Jazz then spawned a variety of sub-genres: New Orleans *Dixieland* dating from 1910, *boogie woogie* and *swing* from the 1930s, *bebop* from the 1940's, and other styles such as *rock'n'roll* and *rhythm & blues*.

In the 1930's, a style of music called *swing* developed that had a smoother rhythm and more sophisticated melodies. It was featured by artists such as Benny Goodman, Duke Ellington, Count Basie, and Glenn Miller who all played *swing*. This was an era when *Big Bands* reigned supreme.

The 1950's to the present day saw numerous other musical genres including *rock'n'roll*, *rhythm & blues*, and *country*. Superstars Mick Jagger, Bruce Springsteen, and many others toured America and world-wide filling stadiums with "rock concerts". From this genesis, modern music developed numerous styles and is carried to many venues throughout America and world-wide.

TWENTY: JAZZ

Jazz started as folk music which came with Black slaves who brought their musical heritage with them when they arrived on slave ships, and it originated in the African-American community of the American South. The slave trade brought almost half a million Africans to America, and they brought strong tribal traditions with them. Its African pedigree is evident in the use of blue notes, improvisation, polyrhythm, syncopation, and the swung note. Festivals featuring African dances to drums occurred on Sundays at *Place Congo* in New Orleans. This tradition made use of a single-line-melody, but without the European concept of harmony. Rhythms that reflected African speech patterns and the use of pentatonic scales led to blue notes in *blues* and *jazz*. [92]

"Jazz has manipulated instruments, pitch, and the human voice in ways to bring an entirely new palette of colors into music." [93] While it may be difficult to define, improvisation is a key element. Early *jazz* was structured around a repetitive call-and-response pattern, a common element in the African American oral tradition and fundamental to this music. It contrasts with the European tradition where the performer plays the music as it was written. In *jazz*, the performer will interpret a tune in very individual ways, never playing the same composition exactly the same way twice, and may interact with fellow musicians or even members of the audience. It is supported by a rhythm section that plays chords and rhythms that outline the song structure, and complement the soloist. [94]

However, there remains debate about *jazz*. Here is from another source, the Britannica Encyclopedia:

> "Any attempt to arrive at a precise, all-encompassing definition of jazz is probably futile. Jazz has been a constantly evolving, expanding, changing music, passing through several distinctive phases of development; a definition that might apply to one phase -- for instance New Orleans style or swing -- become inappropriate when applied to another segment of its history. Early attempts to define jazz as music whose chief characteristic was improvisation turned out to be too restrictive and largely untrue. … Similarly, syncopation and swing are in fact lacking in much authentic jazz. Again, the long-held notion that swing could not occur without syncopation was roundly disproved when trumpeters Louis Armstrong and Bunny Berigan (among others) frequently generated enormous swing while playing repeated, un-syncopated quarter notes." [95]

It appears that the definition of *jazz* is dependent on which segment of its evolution someone is talking about. "European classical music is a composer's medium; *jazz*, however, is the product of interaction and collaboration, placing equal value on the contributions of composer and performer, and weighing the respective claims of the composer and the improviser." [96]

From its beginnings in the early 20th century, *jazz* has spawned many sub-genres: New Orleans *Dixieland* dating from the 1910s, *swing* from the 1930's, *boogie woogie* from the 1940's, *free jazz* from the 1960's, *bebop* from the 1970's, and later influences that added *funk, rap*, and *hip-hop* from the 1980's. As the music spread around the world, its aesthetics have been adapted to varied environments and gave rise to many distinctive styles. [97]

In New Orleans *Dixieland*, performers took turns playing the melody while others improvised counter-melodies. By the *swing* era, *Big Bands* were relying more on arranged music, which was either written or learned by ear and memorized -- many early *jazz* performers could not read music.

There have long been debates over the definition and boundaries of *Jazz*. Alteration has been criticized as a "debasement", but some argue that *jazz* has the ability to transform influences from diverse musical tastes -- suggesting an evolution in style. Musicians themselves are often reluctant to define the music they play. Duke Ellington summed it up by saying, "it's all music." Some critics have even stated that Ellington's music was not *jazz* because it was arranged and orchestrated; on the other hand, the music critic of the *New York Times described it* as "as good an example of *jazz* as anything out there." [98]

The origin of the word *"jazz"* is one of the most sought-after words in modern English. The word's intrinsic interest has resulted in considerable research by the American Dialect Society and its history is well documented. The word began as West Coast slang, the meaning of which varied but did not refer to music or sex; it first came as a reference to music in Chicago around 1915. [99]

In the early 20th century an increasing number of black musicians learned to play instruments, particularly the violin, which they used to parody dance music in their cakewalk dances. In turn, minstrel show performers in blackface popularized such music, combining syncopation with harmonic accompaniment. Another influence came from slaves who incorporated it into their own music as spirituals; the origin of the *blues* can be seen as the secular counterpart of the spirituals.

The abolition of slavery led to new opportunities for African-Americans. Black musicians were able to provide entertainment in dances, minstrel shows, and vaudeville; and Black pianists played in bars, clubs, and brothels as ragtime developed. The classically trained pianist, Scott Joplin, produced his *Original Rags* and an international hit with *Maple Leaf Rag*. He wrote numerous popular rags that combined syncopation, banjo figurations, and call-and-response, which led to the ragtime idiom being taken up by classical composers. *Blues* music was popularized by W.C. Handy, who's *Memphis Blues* and *St Louis Blues* of 1914 both became *jazz* standards. [100]

The music of New Orleans had a profound effect on the creation of early *jazz* and early performers played in venues throughout the city. The brothels and bars of the red-light district around Basin Street were called Storyville, one of numerous neighborhoods of the early days of New Orleans *jazz*. In addition to dance bands, marching bands played at lavish funerals. Vaudeville shows took *jazz* to western and northern US cities. [101]

The *Original Dixieland Jazz Band* made their first recordings in 1917, and their *Livery Stable Blues* became the earliest released *jazz* record. A Dixieland standard is the *Darktown Strutters Ball*. (Every dance in the Buffalo Gap auditorium during my youth included this lively song when it was time for a super-fast *jitterbug* number.) Prohibition in the United States from 1920 to 1933 banned the sale of alcoholic drinks, resulting in illicit speakeasies becoming lively venues of the "Jazz Age". It started to get a reputation as being immoral; the older generation saw it as promoting the decadent values of the Roaring 20's. A Princeton University professor wrote *"...jazz is not music at all. It's merely an irritation of the nerves of hearing, a sensual teasing of the strings of physical passion."* [102] Even the media began to denigrate *jazz*, including the *New York Times* that altered headlines to nit-pick at the style.

In 1924 Louis Armstrong joined the Fletcher Henderson dance band as featured soloist for a year, and then formed his virtuosic *"Hot Five"*. The same year, Whiteman commissioned Gershwin's *Rhapsody in Blue*, which was premièred by his orchestra. Other large ensembles included Duke Ellington's band (which opened in New York in 1927 at the Cotton Club), and Earl Hines's Band in Chicago. All these influenced the development of the *Big Band* style of music. [103]

In the early 1940's during World War Two when many big bands became a causality of the war, *bebop* performers helped to shift *jazz* from danceable popular music towards a "musician's music." *Bebop* divorced itself from dance music, establishing itself more as an art form but lessening its popular and commercial value. Since *bebop* was meant to be listened to, not danced to, it used faster tempos. Beboppers introduced new forms of chromaticism and dissonance into *jazz*. These divergences from the mainstream met with a hostile response among some fans and fellow musicians, especially established *swing* players who bristled at the new harmonic sounds. Despite the initial friction, by the 1950's *bebop* had become an accepted part of the vocabulary.

Some classical composers such as Aaron Copland, Claude Debussy, and Igor Stravinsky were drawn to the instrumental inflections and syncopations of *jazz* -- sounds that musicians make on their instruments -- and incorporated it into their classical compositions. [104]

In the 1980's, the *jazz* community shrank dramatically. An older audience retained an interest in traditional *jazz* styles. Wynton Marsalis, leader of the *Lincoln Center Jazz Orchestra*, strove to create music within what he believed was the tradition, creating extensions of forms initially pioneered by such artists as Louis Armstrong and Duke Ellington. In the 21st century, *jazz* continues to appeal to well-established musicians, such as Dave Brubeck, and Wynton Marsalis who continue to perform and record.

In 1987, the United States Congress passed a bill to define *jazz* as a unique form of American music stating, among other things, *"...that jazz is hereby designated as a rare and valuable national American treasure to which we should devote our attention, support and resources to make certain it is preserved, understood and promulgated."* [105]

In future years we will no-doubt witness the continuing evolution of *jazz*, a distinctly American music art form.

TWENTY ONE: LOUIS (LOUIE) ARMSTRONG

Louis Armstrong was a *jazz* trumpeter from New Orleans who came to prominence in the 1920's and was a foundational influence in *jazz*. With his distinctive gravelly voice, he also became a popular singer. Renowned for his charismatic stage presence and voice almost as much as for his trumpet-playing, his reputation extends well beyond *jazz*, and he is regarded as having had a profound influence on popular music in general.

Armstrong was one of the first African-American entertainers whose skin color was secondary to his amazing talent in an America that was racially divided. It allowed him social access to the upper echelons of society that were highly restricted for a person of color.

The grandson of slaves, Armstrong was born in 1901 into poverty and spent his youth living in a rough neighborhood of New Orleans. His father abandoned the family when Louis was an infant. His mother left Louis and his sister in the care of his grandmother, but at age five he moved back to live with his mother. He brought in some money as a paperboy and also by finding discarded food and selling it to restaurants, but it was not enough to keep his mother from prostitution. For extra money he also hauled coal to Storyville, the famed red-light district, and listened to the bands playing in the brothels and dance halls. After dropping out of school, he joined a quartet of boys that sang in the streets for money. Armstrong did not look back at his youth as the worst of times, but instead drew inspiration from it, "Every time I close my eyes blowing that trumpet of mine -- I look right in the heart of good old New Orleans...It has given me something to live for." [106]

Armstrong started playing the cornet in the band of the *Home for Colored Waifs*, where he had been sent for general delinquency. Eventually, the school director made Armstrong the band leader. The band performed around New Orleans and Louis began to draw attention at the age of thirteen, and he got his first dance hall job, hauling coal by day and playing cornet at night. Later, he played on the riverboats, and began traveling in a steamboat up and down the Mississippi River. He described this time as, "*Going to the* university," since it gave him experience working with written arrangements. [107]

After he married Daisy Parker, they adopted a 3-year-old boy who was mentally disabled (the result of a head injury at an early age), and Louis would spend the rest of his life taking care of him. His marriage to Parker failed, they separated, and she died shortly after the divorce.

With his riverboat experience, Armstrong's musicianship began to mature. At twenty, he could read music and he started to be featured in trumpet solos, injecting his own style. He learned how to create a unique sound and started using singing and patter in his performances. At the age of twenty, Armstrong moved to Chicago to join the Creole Jazz Band where he could make sufficient income and stop working in day labor jobs. The band was the most influential band in Chicago when the city was the center of the jazz universe. Armstrong lived like a king in his own apartment and with his own private bath. At this time, he met Hoagy Carmichael, with whom he would later collaborate.

Armstrong married a second time to Lil Hardin, a piano player, and she became a big influence in his life. Lil had her husband play classical music in church concerts to broaden his skill and improve his solo play, and she prodded him into wearing more stylish attire to make him look sharp. Armstrong received an invitation to go to New York City to play with the Fletcher Henderson Orchestra, the top African-American band of the day. He switched to the trumpet to blend in better with the other musicians in his section and quickly adapted to the more controlled style of Henderson. Soon his act included singing and telling tales about New Orleans characters. Armstrong returned to Chicago because the Henderson Orchestra was limiting his artistic growth. He then had success with vocal recordings, including versions of famous songs composed by his old friend Hoagy Carmichael. His interpretation of Carmichael's Stardust became one of the most successful versions ever recorded, showcasing Armstrong's unique vocal sound and his innovative approach to singing songs that had already become standards. His vocal innovations served as a foundation for the art of *jazz* interpretation; the uniquely gritty coloration of his voice became a musical archetype that was much imitated.

The Great Depression of the thirties was especially hard on musicians. The New York Cotton Club closed in 1936 after a long downward spiral and many musicians stopped playing altogether as club dates evaporated; Armstrong moved to Los Angeles to seek new opportunities. His band drew the Hollywood crowd, which could still afford a lavish night life, while radio broadcasts connected with younger audiences.

Armstrong then began to experience problems with his fingers and lips, which were aggravated by his unorthodox playing style. As a result he branched out, developing his vocal style and making his first theatrical appearances. He appeared in movies, including Bing Crosby's 1936 hit Pennies from Heaven. Armstrong substituted for Rudy Vallee on the CBS radio network and became the first African American to host a national broadcast. He then married longtime girlfriend Alpha, his third marriage. After spending many years on the road, Armstrong settled permanently in New York in 1943 with his fourth wife, Lucille. During the following thirty years, Armstrong had his own band and played more than three hundred gigs a year. Bookings for *Big Bands* tapered off during the 1940's. Ballrooms closed and there was competition from television. It became difficult under such circumstances to support a 16-piece touring orchestra, so he cut back on touring.

In 1964, he recorded his biggest-selling record, "Hello, Dolly!" The song went to #1 on the pop chart, making Armstrong (age 63) the oldest person to ever accomplish that feat. He also dislodged the

Beatles from the #1 position they had occupied for 14 consecutive weeks. Armstrong toured Africa, Europe, and Asia under sponsorship of the U.S. State Department earning the nickname "Ambassador Satch", and kept up his busy schedule until a few years before his death in 1971 at the age of 80. His honorary pallbearers included Bing Crosby, Ella Fitzgerald, Dizzy Gillespie, Pearl Bailey, Count Basie, Harry James, Frank Sinatra, Ed Sullivan, Earl Wilson, Alan King, Johnny Carson and David Frost. Peggy Lee sang The Lord's Prayer at the services. [108]

Armstrong has a star on the Hollywood Walk of Fame on Hollywood Boulevard. He was posthumously awarded the Grammy Lifetime Achievement Award in 1972 by the Academy of Recording Arts and Sciences. Today, there are many bands worldwide dedicated to preserving and honoring the music and style of *Satchmo*, including the Louis Armstrong Society located in New Orleans.

TWENTY TWO: BOOGIE WOOGIE

In my youth prior to World War Two, I heard the music of *boogie woogie*, but do not connect it to any specific style; it was mostly for dancing. When the music in the Buffalo Gap auditorium got fast, real wild and crazy, someone on the dance floor would shout, *"Now, that's real boogie woogie"*.

The Collier's encyclopedia that was written in the 1950's, defines *boogie woogie*: *"A jazz style developed around a short bass figure constantly repeated, either exactly or in sequence (ground bass)."* [109] I don't know enough about music to understand what that means.

The encyclopedia goes on to say, *"Debussy's use of the whole tonal scale ... contributed to the breaking up of the diatonic scale. As a result, the melodic line of Western music was gradually freed from the compulsion of resolving active and passive tones. The whole tone scale with its concomitant harmonies was by 1940 common in the so called 'symphonic' introductions to Boogie Woogie and other kinds of popular music, and could be heard on juke boxes throughout the United States."* [110] That language is technically over-my-head. The words are consistent with the uninhibited behavior historically associated with *boogie woogie* -- but I prefer the Buffalo Gap dance-floor description: *"wild and crazy."*

Boogie-woogie became popular in the late 1930's and is mainly associated with dancing. The lyrics of one of the earliest hits, *"Pinetop's Boogie Woogie"*, consisted entirely of instructions to dancers:

"Now, when I tell you to hold yourself,
Don't you move a peg.
And when I tell you to get it,
I want you to Boogie Woogie."

The origins of boogie woogie occurred in the 1920's in lumber
and turpentine camps in Piney Woods, Texas, where there was a
strong association with the railroad and steam engine. Locomotives
and the building of mainline tracks to serve logging operations
were pivotal to the creation of the music in terms of its sound and
rhythm. [111] The first commercial hit was "Pinetop's Boogie Woogie"
by Pinetop Smith in 1929, and helped establish boogie-woogie as
the name of the style. It was soon followed by Honky Tonk Train
Blues, which emulates a railroad trip. [112] It was played in honky-
tonks on the South Side of Chicago in the 1920's. [113]

Boogie-woogie gained public attention in 1938, thanks to a concert in
Carnegie Hall, *From Spirituals to Swing*. After the Carnegie Hall concert,
swing bands incorporated the *boogie woogie* beat into some of their
music. Tommy Dorsey's band had a hit with an updated version of
Pine Top's Boogie Woogie in 1938. Will Bradley's orchestra had a string
of hits with *Beat Me Daddy (Eight to The Bar)*, *Down the Road A-Piece*,
and *Scrub Me Mamma With A Boogie Beat*. The Andrews Sisters sang
some boogies, and after the floodgates were open, it was expected
that every *Big Band* should have one or two boogie numbers in their
repertoire since the dancers were now learning to *jitterbug*. [114]

Country artists began playing *boogie woogie*. The song *Cow Cow
Boogie* successfully combined it with cowboy music and sold over a
million records. What was called *hillbilly boogie* became popular around
1945 and lasted into the 1950's with records made by Tennessee Ernie
Ford. The boogie beat continued in *country* music through the end of
the 20th century. The Charlie Daniels Band released *Boogie Woogie
Fiddle Country Blues* in 1988, and three years later Brooks & Dunn had
a huge hit with *Boot Scootin' Boogie*. It can also be found in the songs
of country artists such as *Asleep at the Wheel* by Merle Haggard, and
others by George Strait. [115]

The popularity of the Carnegie Hall concerts led to the boogie beat in *Big Bands*. Tommy Dorsey's band had a hit with *T.D.'s Boogie Woogie* and soon there were songs recorded and printed of many different stripes. Most famously, the ubiquitous song, *Boogie Woogie Bugle Boy*, was sung by the Andrew Sisters in a movie by that name. The song was later revamped by Christina Aguilera as her 2006 hit, *Candyman*. [116]

Jamie Foxx won the academy award for his portrayal of Ray Charles in the movie "Ray". Foxx (as Charles) asked if his producers want him to do a "Pete Johnson thing" on the piano while in the recording studio. He then proceeds to play a boogie in the style of the seminal *boogie woogie* musician, Johnson. So while it is a musical genre dating back several decades, it remains very much a part of the modern music scene.

TWENTY THREE: SWING

Swing was my favorite music during my youth in the 1930's, and now seventy-five years later it still is. I developed my first girl-friend "crush" dancing to *swing* music of Glen Miller at Saturday night dances in the Buffalo Gap auditorium. By our standards, that music was damn good. The band was local: Ira Thurston, a garage mechanic, blew the trumpet; Dale Lovell, my 7th grade teacher was on the trombone; Leo Mohler, a cowboy from the Cheyenne River country, strummed the guitar; "Ma Wycoff fingered the piano; Art Ferguson, a rancher from Harrison Flats, was the fiddler; and Jim Nolan, who ran the grain elevator, beat the drums.

Swing is sometimes considered a dilution of *jazz* with written music rather than the improvisatory character of *jazz*; nevertheless, it was the first *jazz* idiom that proved commercially successful. The *swing* era also brought respectability to *jazz*, moving music into the ballrooms of America that until that time had been associated with the brothels of New Orleans and the Prohibition-era gin mills of Chicago." [117]

The Colliers Encyclopedia treats *swing* as only a *jazz* side-show:

> *"Jazz influenced the character of dance music. ... Swing music was heard where true jazz performers played, as, for example, in the Paul Whiteman band that featured men like trombonist Tommy Dorsey and the saxophonist Jimmy Dorsey. ... From those bands came some of the impetus for the second great jazz development -- swing."* [118]

71

A more modern definition is the following from the Wikipedia Encyclopedia:

> *"Swing is a form of jazz music that became a distinctive style by 1935. ... It uses a strong rhythm section as the anchor for a lead section of trumpets, trombones, and saxophones, and sometimes strings instruments such as violin and guitar; with medium to fast tempos and a 'lilting' swing time rhythm. Swing bands usually featured soloists who would improvise on the melody over the arrangement. The danceable swing style of bandleaders such as Benny Goodman, Count Basie, and Glenn Miller was the dominant form of popular music from 1935 to 1945."* [119]

That is how I remember *swing* music.

Swing music used, "edgier" arrangements that emphasized horn instruments and improvised melodies. Louis Armstrong, who would later publicly ridicule *bebop*, shared his version of history. During a broadcast of the Bing Crosby (radio) Show, Armstrong was asked to tell what *swing* music is. Louis said, *"Ah, swing, well, we used to call it ragtime, then blues -- then jazz. Now, it's swing. White folks yo'all sho is a mess. Swing!"* [120]

The overall effect of *swing* was a sophisticated sound, but with an exciting feel of its own. Most *jazz* bands adopted this style by the 1930's, but "sweet" (Black musician) bands remained the most popular for white dancers until Benny Goodman's appearance at the Palomar Ballroom on Catalina Island in August 1935. Goodman's radio show, *Let's Dance*, was on after midnight in the East and few people heard it, but it was on earlier on the West Coast and developed the audience that later led to his Palomar Ballroom triumph. The audience of young white dancers favored Goodman's "hot" rhythms and daring arrangements. [121]

With the wider acceptance of *swing* music around 1935, mainstream bands began to embrace this style of music. Until then, *jazz* had been held in higher regard by most serious musicians around the world, including classical composers like Stravinsky; *swing* was regarded as degeneration and light entertainment -- more of an industry to sell records than a form of art. Many musicians switched to *swing* only after failing at serious music. In his autobiography W.C. Handy wrote:

> *"This brings to mind the fact that prominent white orchestra leaders, concert singers, and others are making commercial use of Negro music in its various phases; that's why they introduced "swing" which is not a musical form."* [122]

Large orchestras had to reorganize themselves in order to achieve the new sound. *Big Bands* dropped their string instruments, which were now felt to hamper the music style. Band leaders began developing arrangements that reduced the chaos that might result from a dozen musicians spontaneously improvising. A typical song would feature a strong rhythm section in support of more loosely tied wind, bass, and string or vocal sections. The most common style consisted of having a soloist take center stage and improvise a solo within the framework of the band playing support. [123]

By the late 1930's, *swing* had become the most popular instrumental style and remained so until it was supplanted in the 1940s by pop standards sung by crooners who grew out of the *Big Band* tradition. Bandleaders such as the Dorsey Brothers often helped launch the careers of vocalists who became popular as solo artists, such as Frank Sinatra.

Swing music began to decline in popularity during World War Two when it became difficult to staff a *Big Band* because many musicians were overseas fighting in the war. Also, the cost of touring with a large ensemble became prohibitive because of wartime economics and smaller combos were more manageable. Another factor is the recording ban of 1942 and 1948 because of musicians' union strikes. In 1948, there were no records legally made at all. When the ban was over in January 1949, *swing* had evolved into new styles such as *bebop*.

Many crooners had their origins in *swing* bands. Frank Sinatra used the music style in almost all of his recordings and kept *swing* popular well into the *rock'n'roll* era. Nat King Cole followed Sinatra into the pop music world, and he was important in bringing piano to the fore of popular music. Artists like Willie Nelson have kept the *swing* elements of country music present into the *rock'n'roll* era. [124]

Rock'n'roll musicians like Fats Domino, Jerry Lee Lewis, Chuck Gerry, Gene Vincent, and Elvis Presley also included *swing*-era standards into their repertoire. Presley's hit *"Are You Lonesome Tonight"* is an old standard, and Lewis's hit *"To Make Love Sweeter For You"* is a new song but in the old style. Fats Domino made the standard *"My Blue Heaven"* a *rock'n'roll* hit.

Although ensembles like the Count Basie Orchestra and the Stan Kenton Orchestra survived into the 1950's by incorporating new musical styles into their repertoire, they were no longer the hallmark of American popular music. In the late 1990's, there was a short-lived "*swing* revival" movement led by bands such as *Big Bad Voodoo Daddy, Speakeasies' Swing Band!, Lavay Smith & Her Red Hot Skillet Lickers, the Lucky strikes,* and *Hipster Daddy-O and the Hand grenades.* Bands of this period played a style of music that combined *swing* with *rock* that blended 1930's dancing with 2000-era styles. A similar approach can be seen with *super-swing* music, a style that had its origin in *The Fabrics'* 2002 classic single *Cassawanka.* [125]

In 2001, Robbie Williams released his album *Swing When You're Winning,* which was popular in many countries worldwide. In 2006, the singer Christina Aguilera released her album *"Back to Basic"* where she mixed different styles including *swing, jazz* and *blues.* The album was another commercial success for Aguilera's career.

The most popular *swing* music in America of the 1930's and 1940's belonged to the *Big Bands,* male "crooners", and female singers. Some soloists became as famous as band leaders. The following are lists of crooners and female singers.

CROONERS

Al Martino, Andrea Bocelli, Bing Crosby, Dick Powell, Bobby Darin, Buddy Greco, Dean Martin, Elvis Presley, Frank Sinatra

Frankie Laine James Darren, Jerry Vale, Julie La Rosa, Louis Prima, Perry Como, Rudy Vallée, Russ Columbo Sammy Davis Jr. Tony Bennett Vic Damone, Mel Tormé, Steve Lawrence, Tony Martin, Eddie Fisher, Harry Connick Jr. Johnny Mathis Johnnie Ray Barry Manilow, Robert Goulet Tom Jones Andy Williams Engelbert Humperdinck, Billy Eckstine Nat King Cole, David Bowie Harry Belefonte, Michael Jackson Fred Astaire Irving Berlin Cole Porter, Roger Williams Pat Boone Vince Gill Eddie Fisher Paul Anka, Lewis Armstrong Julis La Rosa Beatles Paul McCarthy Ringo, Billie Joel Tennessee Ernie Ford Jimmie Dean Nelson Eddie, Bob Dylan Earl Clampton Hoggy Carmichael Kanye West, Ike Turner U2 Sting Steel Four Freshmen The Four Lads, Everly Brothers Alabama Four Aces Mills Brothers, The Platters Ink Spots Bruce Springsteen Jerry Lee Lewis, Little Richard Fats Domino Chuck Berry

FEMALE SINGERS

Equally as important to music of the *swing* era were the female singers. The following list is categorized along several different lines since I could find no single list that included them all. I did not agree with the rankings on some of the lists, and I included only those singers that I am familiar with. I will not repeat names that appear on several lists.

Best female vocalist of all time:

1 Celine Dion	6 Barbara Streisand
2 Mariah Carey	7 Sarah McLachlan
3 Christine Aguilera	8 Alanis Morissette
4 Gladys Knight	9 Aretha Franklin
5 Madonna	10 Tina Turner

Best female vocalists 1970-1998

Ann Murray	Donna Summers	La Toya Jackson
Ginette Reno	Dolly Parton	Alica Keyes
Rita MacNeil	Natalie Cole	Eartha Kitt

Carole Pope   Janet Jackson   Judy Garland
Karen Carpenter   Dianna Ross   Bette Midler
Kay Starr

American Sopranos

Geraldine Farrar   Dorothy Kirsten   Maureen McGovern
Renee Fleming   Patti La Belle   Dolly Parton
Kathryn Grayson   Jeanette Macdonald   Beverly Sills
Roberta Peters

American Contraltos

Cher   Jane Froman   Peggy Lee
Melissa Etheridge Patsy Cline   Lady Gaga
Sarah Vaughan

American Mezzo-Sopranos

Sheryl Crow   Amy Grant   Whitney Houston
Ethel Merman   Selena   Julie London

African American Female

Tyra Banks   Roberta Flack   Carmen McRae
Natalie Cole   Billie Holiday   Pointer Sisters
Dorothy Dandridge Jennifer Hudson   Queen Latifah
Ella Fitzgerald   Eartha Kitt   Phylicia Rashad
Nicole Richie   Donna Summer   Ethel Waters

Other American Pop Singers (not listed above)

Britney Spears   Connie Francis   Doris Day
Shana Twain   Patti Page   Connie Francis
Ann Wilson   Jane Fromen   Debbie Reynolds
Sarah Brightman   Peggy Lee   Rosemary Clooney
Beyonce   Jeanette MacDonald   Andrew Sisters
Dionne Warwick   Dinah Shore   Faith Hill
Dinah Shore   Carry Underwood   Brenda Lee
Theresa Brewer   Julie Andrews

TWENTY FOUR: BIG BANDS

I am biased; my favorite *Big Bands* are those of Glenn Miller and Lawrence Welk.

Glenn Miller is one of greats in modern music, arising to fame near the end of the 1930's Great Depression. World War Two started at the height of his musical career and his music is symbolic of that era. When the war started, he immediately joined the military and entertained the troops in Europe in his role as a captain in the army.

The Lawrence Welk band may not be on "critics' lists"; however, Welk has captivated audiences with his music for over eighty years; and I have personally enjoyed his music during seventy years of my own lifetime. During the 1930's Great Depression, I attended the *Water Carnival* in Hot Springs, South Dakota, with my parents where the Lawrence Welk band was the featured event. In terms of musical excellence and longevity, his band has to be included near the top of any list -- he is virtually the last survivor of the *Big Band* era and almost the only exposure children of the current generation have to this kind of music.

The *Big Band* is a type of musical ensemble that became popular during the *swing* era from the early 1930's until the late 1950's. It typically consisted of 12 to 25 musicians and contained trumpets, saxophones, trombones, singers and a rhythm section. In contrast to smaller jazz combos in which most of the music is improvised or created spontaneously, music played by *Big Bands* is "arranged" and notated on sheet music. Improvised solos may be played only when called for by the arranger. [126]

Big Bands evolved slowly over a couple decades. The first era began in the 1920's when bands came to dominate popular music. They played a form of *jazz* that involved little improvisation and included a string section with violins. Orchestras tended to stick to the melody as it was written and vocals would be sung in tune with the melody. Typical of this genre were such popular artists as Paul Whiteman, Ted Lewis, Rudy Vallee, and Fred Waring. There were also "all-girl" bands such as Helen Lewis and her *All-Girl Jazz Syncopators*. Lewis and her band were filmed in 1925 in three short films which are now in the Library of Congress film collection.

The era of the big bands that began during the 1930's became the most popular and included bands of Benny Goodman, the Dorsey Brothers, Glenn Miller, and many others. (You can see a list of Bandleaders at the end of this chapter.) That is the era that played such a big role in my life. During college in the late 1940's, I danced to the music of the Glenn Miller band after it had been taken over by Tex Beneke. When I was in the navy in the 1950's, I danced to the music of Jimmy Dorsey at the Palladium Ballroom in Santa Monica. In the 1960's, my wife and I listened to the bands of Duke Ellington, Les Brown, and Count Basie in casino lounges in Las Vegas, and also the singer, Ella Fitzgerald. In the 1970's, my entire family and I attended a concert by Woody Herman in Toledo, Ohio, where he was featured as the "Last of the *Big Bands*." He virtually was, except for the orchestra of Lawrence Welk.

Big Bands played a huge role in radio. Earl "Fatha" Hines broadcast live from Chicago with his *Grand Terrace Cafe* band from coast-to-coast. In Kansas City, an earthier style was developed by bandleaders Benny Moten and Jesse Stone. Radio networks spread the music from ballrooms and clubs across the country during the 1930's and 1940's with broadcasts continuing into the 1950's on N.B.C.'s *Monitor*. Radio was a major factor in gaining fame for Benny Goodman, known as the "*King of Swing*". Soon others challenged him, and the *Battles of the Bands* became a staple at performances featuring many groups on one bill.

Big Bands also began to appear in movies in the 1930's. Shep Fields and his orchestra appeared in *The Big Broadcast of 1938* for Paramount Pictures while accompanying the actor Bob Hope. Alvino Rey and His Orchestra were featured in films by RKO Pictures in the early 1940's in such movies as *Sing Your Worries Away*. The Andrew Sisters were in the movie, *Boogie Woogie Bugle Boy*. Fictionalized biographical films of Glenn Miller, Gene Krupa, Benny Goodman, and others were made in the 1950's as nostalgic tributes to the glory years. [127]

Swing music played a major role. *Big Bands* rose to prominence playing this music and there were many different styles among the hundreds of popular bands. Some of the better known ones reflected the individuality of the bandleader and his music. Count Basie played a relaxed propulsive *swing*, Bob Crosby more of a *Dixieland* style, Benny Goodman a hard driving *swing*, and Duke Ellington's compositions were varied and sophisticated. Many bands featured strong instrumentalists whose sounds dominated, such as the clarinets of Benny Goodman, Artie Shaw, and Woody Herman; the trumpets of Jack Teagarden and Harry James; the drums of Gene Krupa, and vibes of Lionel Hampton. The popularity of many of the major bands was amplified by star vocalists such as Frank Sinatra with Tommy Dorsey, Helen O'Connell and Bob Eberly with Jimmy Dorsey, Ella Fitzgerald with Chick Webb, Billie Holiday and Jimmy Rushing with Count Basie, Dick Haymes and Helen Forrest with Harry James, Doris Day with Les Brown, Toni Arden and Ken Curtis with Shep Fields, and Peggy Lee with Benny Goodman. Some bands relied on ensembles rather than vocalists such as the bands of Guy Lombardo and Paul Whiteman. [128]

Big Bands were such a dominant force that the older generation of musicians found they either had to adapt to it or simply retire. Louis Armstrong and Earl Hines then fronted their own bands, while others like Jelly Roll Morton and King Oliver lapsed into obscurity.

Teenagers and young adults were the principal fans of the *Big Bands* in the late 1930's and early 1940's. They danced to recordings, listened to the radio and attended live concerts, were knowledgeable and biased toward their favorite bands, and worshiped the famous soloists and vocalists. Many bands toured the country in grueling one-night stands to reach out to their fans. Traveling conditions and lodging were often difficult, in part due to segregation in parts of the United States, and the personnel often had to perform on little sleep and food. Apart from the star soloists, many personnel received low wages and would abandon the tour and go home if bookings fell through. Personal problems and intra-band discord could affect the playing of the group. Drinking and addictions were common. Turnover was frequent in many bands, and top soloists were often lured away to better contracts. Sometimes bandstands were too small, public address systems inadequate, and pianos out of tune. Successful bandleaders dealt with all these hazards of touring to hold their bands together -- some with rigid discipline (Glenn Miller); some with canny psychology (Duke Ellington).

Big Bands played a major role in lifting morale during World War Two. Many band members served in the military and toured with USO troupes at the front. Then as the war progressed, the *Big Band* era fell into decline. An ill-timed recording strike in 1942 worsened the situation. Vocalists began to strike out on their own and *swing* was giving way to less danceable music including *bebop*. Many of the bands broke up as tastes changed; however, a few exhibitions did occur during the post-war, which included performances by Dizzy Gillespie, Gene Krupa, Buddy Rich, Stan Kenton, and Wynton Marsalis. The *Jazz at Lincoln Center Orchestra* with Wynton Marsalis is the resident orchestra in New York City at Lincoln Center and tours internationally, promoting the *Big Band* sound. [129]

Of course, I still listen every Saturday evening to the *Big Band* of Lawrence Welk that is featured on PBS (Public Broadcasting System's TV). It is my favorite music hour of the week.

Here is a list of *Big Band* Leaders. I hope your favorites are included.

BIG BAND LEADERS

Artie Shaw and His Orchestra	Alvino Rey Orchestra
Benny Goodman and Orchestra	Bob Crosby and the Bob Cats

The Buddy Rich Big Band

Chick Webb and His Orchestra

Count Basie and His Orchestra

Dorsey Brothers Orchestra

The Earl Hines Orchestra

Fletcher Henderson and His Orchestra

Glenn Miller Orchestra

Jack Teagarden and His Orchestra

Stan Kenton and His Orchestra

Louis Armstrong and Orchestra

Lincoln Center Jazz Orchestra

Paul Whiteman

Ray Eberle and His Orchestra

Tommy Dorsey and His Orchestra

Woody Herman and His Big Band

Cab Calloway and His Orchestra

Charlie Spivak and His Orchestra

Dizzy Gillespie and His Orchestra

Duke Ellington and His Orchestra

Eddy Duchin and His Orchestra

Gene Krupa

Guy Lombardo and his Orchestra

Jimmy Dorsey and His Orchestra

Kay Kyser

Lionel Hampton and His Orchestra

Les Brown and Band of Renown

Quincy Jones and His Orchestra

The Tex Beneke Orchestra

Tex Williams

Ziggy Elman and His Orchestra

TWENTY FIVE: GLENN MILLER

Glenn Miller was a leading musician, arranger, composer, and bandleader in the swing era. He was one of the best-selling recording artists from 1939 to 1943, leading one of the most popular Big Bands. Miller's recordings have become standards in the American repertoire and include *In the Mood, American Patrol, Chattanooga Choo Choo, A String of Pearls, Tuxedo Junction, Moonlight Serenade, Little Brown Jug* and *Pennsylvania 6-5000*.

Miller was born on a farm in Iowa in 1904. The family moved to Fort Morgan, Colorado, where Miller went to high school. He became interested in a new style of music called "dance band music," and was so taken with it that he formed his own band with some classmates. By the time Miller graduated from high school in 1921, he had decided to become a professional musician. [130]

Miller entered the University of Colorado at Boulder (my alma mater) where he joined Sigma Nu Fraternity. (Their house was located down the hill from my fraternity, Delta Sigma Phi. Robert Redford also attended the University {a few years after me} and was a member of the Kappa Sigs. All three of our fraternities were considered by sorority girls in the "lower social status" on campus.) Miller spent most of his time away from school, attending auditions and playing any gigs he could get. He dropped out of school after failing three out of five classes one semester, and decided to concentrate on making a career as a professional musician. Miller toured with several groups, eventually landing a spot with a band in Los Angeles. In 1928, when the band arrived in New York City, he sent for and married his college sweetheart, Helen Burger. Miller played in the pit bands of two Broadway shows, *Strike Up the Band* and *Girl Crazy*, where his band mates included Benny Goodman and Gene Krupa.

Glenn Miller formed his first band in 1937. The band failed to distinguish itself from the many others of the era and eventually broke up. Benny Goodman later said,

> "In late 1937, before his band became popular, we were both playing in Dallas. Glenn was pretty dejected, came to see me, and asked, 'What do you do? How do you make it?' I said, 'I don't know, Glenn. You just stay with it.' "

Discouraged, Miller realized that he needed to develop a unique sound. He decided to make the clarinet play a melodic line with a tenor saxophone holding the same note, while three other saxophones harmonized within a single octave.

> "This tone and way of playing provided a fullness and richness so distinctive that none of Miller's imitators could ever accurately reproduce the sound." [131]

With this new sound, he found a way to differentiate his band's style from the many others that existed in the late thirties. Miller talked about his style in the 1939 issue of *Metronome* magazine.

> "You'll notice today some bands use the same trick on every introduction; others repeat the same musical phrase as a modulation into a vocal ... We're fortunate that our style doesn't limit us to stereotyped intros, modulations, first choruses, endings or even trick rhythms. The fifth sax, playing clarinet most of the time, lets you know whose band you're listening to. And that's about all there is to it." [132]

The band began a huge rise in popularity, and Time *Magazine* noted:

"Of the twelve to 24 discs in each of today's 300,000 U.S. jukeboxes, from two to six are usually Glenn Miller's." Miller's huge success culminated with his band appearing at Carnegie Hall along with bands of Paul Whiteman, Benny Goodman, and Fred Waring.

For three years prior to the war, Miller's band was featured three times a week during a broadcast with the Andrews Sisters. His first gold record was *Chattanooga Choo-Choo*, performed with his singers "Tex" Beneke, Ray Eberle, Paula Kelly and the vocal group, the Modernaires. Miller and his band appeared in two Twentieth Century Fox films, including the hit *Sun Valley Serenade*.

After World War Two broke out and at the peak of his career, Miller decided to join the war effort. At 38, he was too old to be drafted and volunteered for the Navy, but was told that they did not need his services. He persuaded the United States Army to accept him so he could, in his own words, *"be placed in charge of a modernized Army band."*

Miller's attempts at modernizing military music were met with resistance from career officers. This led to permission for him to form a 50-piece Army Air Force Band and take it to England in the summer of 1944, where he gave 800 performances. While in England, Major Miller recorded a series of songs with the American singer Dinah Shore. In summarizing Miller's military career, General Jimmy Doolittle said, *"next to a letter from home, that organization was the greatest morale builder in the European Theater of Operations."* [133]

On December 15, 1944, Miller was to fly from England to Paris and play for the soldiers there. His single engine plane disappeared while flying over the English Channel. No trace of the plane has ever been found. Miller's status is listed as "missing in action". He left behind his wife, the former Helen Burger originally from Boulder, Colorado, and two children. Helen Miller accepted the Bronze Star medal posthumously for Glenn in February 1945.

Many regard the sound of his orchestra as the definitive popular music of its time. The orchestra was held together for a time after the war under saxophonist Tex Beneke, and it eventually became the *Tex*

Beneke Orchestra. [134] Future composer Henry Mancini was the band's pianist and one of the arrangers.

After Miller's disappearance, the *Army Air Force Band* was decommissioned and the European theater put together another band, the *314*, to take its place. According to singer Tony Bennett, who sang with it while he was in the service, the *314* was the immediate successor to the Glenn Miller led A.A.F. orchestra.

Glenn Miller was accorded numerous honors after his death. In 1953, Universal-International pictures released The Glenn Miller Story, starring James Stewart as the lead. In 1996, the U.S. Postal Service issued a Glenn Miller postage stamp. The National Academy of Recording Arts and Sciences (Grammys), honored Glenn Miller by including three of his recordings in their Hall of Fame: *In The Mood, Moonlight Serenade*, and *Chattanooga Choo Choo*"; and in 2003, Miller posthumously received the Grammy Lifetime Achievement Award.

TWENTY SIX: LAWRENCE WELK

Lawrence Welk was a bandleader who hosted The Lawrence Welk Show on TV beginning in 1955, and it is still being performed five decades later on PBS, the Public Broadcasting System. His style came to be known to his fans as "champagne music."

Welk was born in 1903 in the German-speaking community of Strasburg, North Dakota. He was sixth of the eight children of Ludwig and Christiana Welk, ethnic Germans who immigrated to America from Odessa, Ukraine. The family lived on a homestead and spent the cold North Dakota winter of their first year under an upturned wagon covered in sod.

Welk decided on a career in music and persuaded his father to buy a mail-order accordion for $400. He promised his father that he would work on the farm until he was 21 in repayment, and any money he made during that time doing farm work or performing would go to his family. Welk began learning English as soon as he started school. The part of North Dakota where he lived had been settled by Germans from Russia and his teachers spoke English as a second language: Welk thus acquired his trademark accent. He took elocution lessons in the 1950's and could speak almost accent-free, but he realized his public expected to hear him say: *"A-one, an-a-two"* and *"Wunnerful, Wunnerful!"* [135]

On his 21st birthday, having fulfilled his promise to his father, Welk left the family farm to pursue a career in music. During the 1920's, he performed with several other bands before starting his own. He led bands that included the *Hotsy Totsy Boys* and the *Honolulu Fruit Gum Orchestra*. His was also the station band for WNAX in Yankton, South Dakota

During the 1930's, Welk led a band that specialized in dance music. Initially, the band traveled around the country by car; but they were too poor to rent rooms, so usually slept and changed clothes in their cars. The band played an annual "gig" at the *Hot Springs Water Carnival*, a "big deal" for us who lived nearby in Buffalo Gap. As a small boy, I accompanied my parents and family for the drive to Hot Springs in our Model A Ford to listen to the band.

The term "Champagne Music" was derived from an engagement at the William Penn Hotel in Pittsburgh, when a dancer referred to his band's sound as "light and bubbly as champagne." In the 1940's, the band began a 10-year stint at the Trianon Ballroom in Chicago, regularly drawing crowds of nearly 7,000. His orchestra also performed frequently at the Roosevelt Hotel in New York City. For two years, the band had its own national radio program sponsored by "The Champagne of Bottle Beer" Miller High Life. [136]

Welk then moved to Los Angeles, where *The Lawrence Welk Show*, a program of band music with vocalists, dancers, and featured soloists, helped make him one of the wealthiest performers in show business. He maintained a roster of musical regulars, including the Champagne Lady (vocalist Alice Lon, followed by Norma Zimmer) and the Lennon Sisters. When the network dropped the program, he contracted with more than 250 independent television stations in the United States and Canada to continue broadcasting -- on TV for nearly six decades. Welk titled his two autobiographies after his trademark phrases, *Wunnerful, Wunnerful!* (1971) and *Ah-One, Ah-Two!* (1974). [137]

Welk's television program had a policy of playing well known songs so the audience would hear only numbers with which they were familiar. The type of music concentrated on popular music standards, polkas, and novelty songs, delivered in a smooth, calm, good-humored easy listening style and "family-oriented" manner. Although described by one critic as "*the squarest music this side of Euclid,* this strategy proved successful and the show remained on the air long after other *Big Bands* had disappeared.

Much of the show's appeal was Welk himself. His accent was popular with the audience. While Welk's English was passable, he never did grasp the English "idiom" completely and was thus famous for his "Welk-isms," such as *"George, I want to see you when you have a minute, right now"* and *"Now for my accordion solo; Myron, will you join me?"* Another "Welk-ism" was his trademark count-off, *"A one and a two . . . ,"* which was immortalized on his California automobile license plate that read "A1ANA2."

He often took women from the audience for a turn around the dance floor. During one show, Welk brought a cameraman out to dance with one of the women and took over the camera himself. Welk's musicians were always top quality, including accordionist Myron Floren, concert violinist Dick Kesner, guitarist Buddy Merrill, and New Orleans Dixieland clarinetist Pete Fountain. Though Welk was occasionally rumored to be very tight with a dollar, he paid his regular band members top scale -- a very good living for a working musician. Long tenure was common among the regulars, and he was noted for spotlighting individual members of his band. Welk had a number of hits, including "Calcutta". Welk himself was indifferent to the tune, but his musical director, George Cates, said that if Welk did not wish to record the song, he (Cates) would. Welk replied, *"Well, if it's good enough for you, George, I guess it's good enough for me." Calcutta* reached number 1 on the pop charts in 1961, and was recorded in only one take. The albums *Last Date, Yellow Bird, Moon River, Young World, Calcutta,* and *"Baby Elephant Walk* were in Billboard's top ten; nine more albums were in the top twenty. [138]

Welk's insistence on wholesome entertainment led him to be a somewhat stern taskmaster at times. For example, he fired Alice Lon, the show's "Champagne Lady," because she was showing too much leg. Welk told the audience that he would not tolerate such "cheesecake" performances on his show; he later tried unsuccessfully to rehire the singer after fan mail indicated overwhelmingly that viewers disagreed with her dismissal. He then had a series of short-term "Champagne

Ladies" before Norma Zimmer filled that spot on a permanent basis. Highly involved with his stars' personal lives, he often arbitrated their marriage disputes.

The Lawrence Welk Show embraced changes on the musical scene over the years. The show featured fresh music alongside the classics, even music originally not intended for the *Big Band* sound. For instance, the show incorporated material by the Beatles, Burt Bacharach and Hal David, the Everly Brothers and *Paul Williams*. A.B.C. cancelled the show in the spring of 1971, citing an aging audience. Welk thanked A.B.C. and the sponsors at the end of the last show; and then continued *The Lawrence Welk Show* as a syndicated show on 250 stations across the country, and it is still carried today on P.B.S. (the Public Broadcasting System).

Welk was married for 61 years, until his death, to Fern Renner, with whom he had three children. One of his sons, Lawrence Welk Jr., married performer Tanya Falan; they later divorced. Welk had many grandchildren and great-grandchildren. Welk enjoyed playing golf and was often a regular at celebrity pro-ams such as the Los Angelis Open. (My wife and I visited with him there after he completed the eighteenth hole when he was one of the celebrity players.) A devout, life-long Roman Catholic, Welk was a daily communicant. Welk died from pneumonia in Santa Monica, California in 1992 at age 89.

He received a number of honors. In 1961, he was inducted as a charter member of the Rough Rider Award from his native North Dakota. He served as the Grand Marshal for the Rose Bowl's Tournament of Roses parade in 1977. In 1994, he was inducted into the International Polka Music Hall of Fame. He has a star on the Hollywood Walk of Fame, located at 6613½ Hollywood Blvd.

TWENTY SEVEN: BEBOP

Bebop is a style of jazz characterized by fast tempo, instrumental virtuosity and improvisation that first surfaced during the Second World War. Also called *"bop"*, it split *jazz* into opposing camps -- between older and younger musicians -- and the breach never completely healed.

We seldom heard *bebop* music in Buffalo Gap. It was not carried on KOBH radio out of Rapid City, nor do I recall any recordings of the style; not that anyone in town other than the Nolan's had a Motorola record player, and I'm sure the Nolan's never listened to that style of music. We would have considered *bebop* as some sort of new craze coming out of the East Coast -- where all those silly crazes began.

Bebop had a strange beginning. As previously discussed in a previous chapter on *Big Bands*, the large orchestras nearly disappeared as a casualty of the war. Many band members were drafted into the army and most dance parlors were now empty. Within this wartime climate, a cadre of young band members started this new genre called *bebop* that featured instrumental music as opposed to danceable *swing* music. They found receptive listeners for music half-scored and half-improvised. In spite of the strong opposition of those who preferred *swing*, the day of "modern jazz" had begun. [139]

Bebop was developed by the saxophonist Charlie Parker and the trumpeter Dizzy Gillespie. The progressive bands of Stan Kenton and

Woody Herman absorbed the major elements of this new style in their arrangements. As described in Collier's encyclopedia,

> *"Attempts were made to get away from music more harmonic than melodic in its character, and a new emphasis was placed on the long melodic line. Rhythmically, too, bop supported even accents. This music hotly supported by its performers and followers, was just as vigorously condemned by those who favored a revival of New Orleans or Dixieland jazz. "* [140]

Bebop helped to shift *jazz* from danceable music towards "musician's music." It divorced itself from dance, establishing itself as an art form, which lessened its commercial value. Since it was meant to be listened to, not danced to, it used faster tempos. Musicians introduced new styles; the "dissonant triton" became an important interval, and players engaged in a more chord-based improvisation. The cymbal was used to keep time, while the snare and bass drum were used for accents. These divergences from the *jazz* mainstream met with a hostile response among fans that bristled at the new sounds. Despite the initial friction, by the 1950's *bebop* had become an accepted part of the vocabulary. [141]

In later years most of the controversy concerning *bebop* subsided. Schools of *jazz* continued to exist but with less rigorous guarding of the lines of distinction. Performances of a classical nature by composers such as Stravinsky and Schonberg included elements of the style. Dave Brubeck brought classical *jazz* concepts with the techniques necessary to express them. While *bebop* music is seldom played, it had a definite impact on the future of *jazz*. At the same time, there has been a growing consciousness on the part of musicians of the roots of *jazz*; and they are expressing them in revivals of *Dixieland,* and a return to the accented rhythm of *swing.* [142]

TWENTY EIGHT: RHYTHM & BLUES

Just as some other styles of music were not named until long after they first appeared, that is also the case with *rhythm & blues*. The Collier Encyclopedia from the 1950's did not contain any reference to this music by name, and only referred to songs that were later to be assigned to the *R&B* genre. [143]

The term was originally used by record companies to describe recordings marketed to African Americans at a time when "rocking, jazz music with a heavy beat" was becoming more popular. The term *R&B* was used to refer to styles that incorporated *blues* as well as *gospel* and *soul* music. [144]

Billboard magazine coined the term *rhythm & blues* in 1948 as a marketing term. It replaced the term "race music", which originally came from within the black community, but was deemed offensive in the postwar world. The term continues to categorize music made by black musicians, as distinct from styles of music made by other musicians. [145]

An "R&B Top Stars of 56" tour took place with the headliner Carl Perkins, whose "*Blue Suede Shoes*" was popular with R&B music buyers. The tour was hugely popular. Perkins said there was a lot of rioting going on: "*just crazy, man! The music drove 'em insane.*" In Annapolis 70,000 people tried to attend a sold out performance with 8,000 seats. Roads were clogged for seven hours. [146]

By the mid-1950s, the distinction between *rock'n'roll* and *rhythm &*

blues was not based on any hard-and-fast rules, and most performers issued records that fit in both categories. One important figure in this transition was Ike Turner, a piano-player-turned-guitarist who fronted a band called the *Kings of Rhythm*. When Turner married the former Anna Mae Bullock and rechristened her Tina Turner, the *Ike and Tina Turner Revue* became a significant force in the modernization of *rhythm & blues*.

By 1960, *rhythm & blues* was, if not a spent force, at least aging with its audience. Performers were appearing more in nightclubs than in revues in which they had made their names. Significantly, in the 1969 issue of *Billboard,* the name was changed, to *soul*. Although *soul* then became the preferred term for black popular music, in some quarter's *rhythm & blues* continued to be used to refer to nearly every genre of post-World War black music. [147]

Film makers took advantage of the popularity of *rhythm & blues*. Little Richard, Chuck Berry, Fats Domino, Big Joe Turner, The Treniers, The Platters, The Flamingos, all made it onto the big screen. Three Elvis Presley records made the *R&B* top five in 1957: *Jailhouse Rock, Treat Me Nice*, and *All Shook Up*. Nat King Cole, a former *jazz* pianist on the pop charts in the early 1950's (*Mona Lisa* and *Too Young*), had a record in the *R&B* charts in 1958, *Looking Back/Do I Like It*.

British *rhythm & blues* developed in the early 1960s, largely as a response to the recordings of American artists. Most successful were the *Rolling Stones*, whose first album in 1964 largely consisted of *rhythm & blues* standards. They became the second most popular UK band (after *The Beatles*) and led a second wave of the "British Invasion" of the US pop charts. Blues songs and influences continued to surface in the *Rolling Stones'* music to this day.

TWENTY NINE: JITTERBUG MUSIC

While *jitterbug* is a dance and not a style of music, per se, the repertoire of songs used for the dance became known as "*jitterbug* music" -- at least among my Edgemont High School generation. At high school dances in the 1940's, we played two kinds of music on the juke box: *jitterbug* and *swing*.

Jitterbug was popular in the 1930's and '40's. Its freewheeling swings and lifts were sometimes almost acrobatic, but were modified for more conservative dancers (such as me). Couples did most versions while holding one or both hands. Step patterns varied widely and included such dances as *jive* and the *lindy hop*. For the *jive* version, dancers took a step to each side and then executed two "shuffles". In the *lindy hop* (named for Charles Lindbergh and popular before my time), the dancers usually did two slow "dig" steps and two quicksteps. *Jitterbug* music -- also called *jive* -- is in $^4/_4$ time with syncopated rhythm. [148]

Editions of Arthur Murray's 1959 book, "How to Become a Good Dancer" contain the following text:

> "There are hundreds of regional dances of the "Jitterbug" type. Formerly called Jitterbug, Lindy Hop and various other names in different parts of the country. ... Swing is the newer title". [149]

The term *jitterbug* comes from an early 20th-century slang term used to describe alcoholics who suffered from the "jitters" (i.e., delirium tremens). In popular culture, it became to mean a type of swing dance

-- "they danced *the jitterbug*", or the act of dancing --"People were jitterbugging, jumping around, cutting loose and going crazy". [150]

Cab Calloway's 1934 recording of *Call of the Jitter Bug* and the film *Cab Calloway's Jitterbug Party* popularized use of the word "jitterbug". Lyrics clearly demonstrate the association between the word and the consumption of alcohol:

> *If you'd like to be a jitter bug,*
>
> *First thing you must do is get a jug,*
>
> *Put whiskey, wine and gin within,*
>
> *And shake it all up and then begin.*
>
> *Grab a cup and start to toss,*
>
> *You are drinking jitter sauce!*
>
> *Don't you worry, you just mug,*
>
> *And then you'll be a jitter bug!* [151]

In the 1947 film *Hi De Ho*, Calloway includes the following lines in his song *Minnie the Moocher*:

> *"Woe there ain't no more Smokey Joe*
>
> *She's fluffed off his hi-de-ho*
>
> *She's a solid jitterbug*
>
> *And she starts to cut a rug*
>
> *Oh! Minnie's a hep cat now."* [152]

The shag and lindy represented the earlier basics of *jitterbug*, which gave way to the *double lindy*. [153]

> *"In jitterbug the hardest thing to learn is the pelvic motion. Those motions are somehow obscene. You have to sway, forwards and backwards, with a controlled hip movement, while your shoulders stay level and your feet glide along the floor. Your right hand is*

held low on the girl's back, and your left hand down at your side, enclosing her hand." [154]

A number called "The Jitterbug" was written for the 1939 film *The Wizard of Oz*. The *jitterbug* was a bug sent by the Wicked Witch of the West to waylay the heroes by forcing them to do a *jitterbug*-style dance. Although the sequence was not included in the final version of the film, the Witch is later heard to tell the flying monkey leader, "I've sent a little insect on ahead to take the fight out of them." The song as sung by Judy Garland as Dorothy and some of the establishing dialogue survived from the soundtrack as the B-side of the disc release of *Over the Rainbow*. [155]

In 1957, the Philadelphia-based television show American Bandstand was carried by A.B.C. It featured popular songs, live appearances by musicians, and dancing. The most popular fast dance was *jitterbug*, which was described as "*a frenetic leftover of the swing era ballroom days that was only slightly less acrobatic than Lindy*." [156]

While the dance is still re-created by old timers (like me when we have a cocktail and are caught out on the dance floor during a fast number), it is gradually becoming known by the younger set as something from ancient times.

THIRTY: CONTEMPORARY FOLK MUSIC

Folk music encompasses both traditional and contemporary folk music. Since I was never a fan of traditional *folk* music, which may have been historically interesting but not melodic and rather boring, I shall focus on contemporary *folk* music that came to prominence primarily as protest music during the Vietnam War and Civil Rights movement.

The "second folk revival" of the 20th century brought a new contemporary genre of popular music marketed by recordings, broadcasting, and concerts. One of the earliest figures in this revival was Woody Guthrie who collected *folk* music in the 1930's and 1940's and also composed his own songs; as did Pete Seeger in the 1930's, Jimmie Rodgers in the 1940's, Burl Ives in the early 1950's, Harry Belafonte in the 1950's, and The Kingston Trio and The Limeliters in the 1960's. Here is a review of some of these. [157]

Woody Guthrie (1912 –1967) was a singer and songwriter whose legacy includes hundreds of political and traditional songs and ballads. His best-known song is This Land Is Your Land. Guthrie traveled with migrant workers and learned traditional folk and blues songs. Many of his songs are about the Dust Bowl era during the Great Depression.

Burl Ives (1909-1995) dropped out of college to travel around as an itinerant singer during the early 1930's, earning his way by doing odd jobs and playing his banjo. In the 1940's he had his own radio show, titled *The Wayfaring Stranger*. Ives was cast as a singing cowboy in the film *Smoky in 1946*. You may also remember him as the voice for *Rudolph the Red Nosed Raindeer*.

Pete Seeger met Woody Guthrie at a "Grapes of Wrath" migrant workers' concert in 1940, and the two thereafter began a musical collaboration.

Harry Belafonte started his career as a club singer. At first he was a pop singer, but later developed an interest in *folk* music. His album *Calypso* (1956) was the first to sell a million copies, and Belafonte was dubbed the "King of Calypso."

The Kingston Trio was formed in 1957 in Palo Alto, California by Bob Shane, Nick Reynolds, and Dave Guard, who were just out of college. They became the most popular singing group of their time.

The Limeliters are a folk music group, formed in 1959 by Lou Gottlieb, Alex Hassilev, and Glenn Yarbrough, and was active until 1965, when they disbanded. After a hiatus of sixteen years they reunited and began performing again and are still performing, but with without any of the original members.

Joan Baez's career started in 1958 at age 17 when she gave her first coffee-house concert. She performed at the Newport Folk Festival and gained renown for her clear voice and three-octave range. In the early 1960's, Baez moved into the forefront of "protest music" for the anti-Vietnam War movement. Her personal convictions -- peace, social justice, anti-poverty -- were reflected in the songs of her repertoire, and Baez became a symbol for these particular concerns. (As a side note, Baez was married for a short time to Harvey, who owned Harvey's Casino in South Lake Tahoe; and my Brother, Dennis, managed a herd of cattle for Harvey when Dennis was manager of a diary in Genoa, Nevada.)

Bob Dylan often performed and toured with Joan Baez. As Baez adopted some of Dylan's songs into her repertoire and introduced Dylan to her audiences, it helped the young songwriter gain recognition. He wrote songs that captured the "progressive" mood on the college campuses, and became the most popular of these younger folk music performers.

Peter, Paul and Mary debuted in the early 1960's and they were a trio who became one of the biggest musical acts of the 1960's. The trio was composed of Peter Yarrow, Paul Stookey and Mary Travers. They were one of the main torchbearers of social commentary folk music in the 1960's.

Judy Collins debuted in the early 1960's. She sang folk songs written by others -- in particular the protest poets of the time, such as Tom Paxton, Phil Ochs, and Bob Dylan.

Smothers Brothers: Tom and Dick Smothers were singers and comedians. Their 'trademark act" was performing folk songs that usually led to arguments between the siblings. Tommy's signature line was, *"Mom always liked you best!"* Tommy (the elder of the two) acted "slow", and Dick, the straight man, acted "superior". Their television variety show,

The Smothers Brothers Comedy Hour, became one of the most controversial of the Vietnam War era. Despite popular success, the brothers' penchant for material that was critical of the political mainstream and sympathetic to the emerging counter-culture led to their firing by the CBS network in 1969. The brothers continued to work on stage, television, and in films during subsequent decades.

The political "protest music" of the anti-Vietnam war movement occurred during the 1960's with performers such as Bob Dylan, Joan Baez, and Judy Collins. Others followed expressing support for various causes including the American Civil Rights Movement and anti-war causes associated with the Vietnam War. The Smothers Brothers television shows featured many *folk* performers, including formerly blacklisted ones such as Pete Seeger and Harry Belafonte. [158]

The 1960's era was a turbulent time in America. At that time, I was manager in a factory in Oakland. To get to work I had to drive through race riots occurring two blocks away in East 14th street. Inside the factory, we had more of the same on a lesser scale. On Sunday, I drove my family to church in Berkeley through street barricades manned by National Guard troops who were maintaining Martial Law. My novel, *1960s DECADE OF DISSENT: The Way We Were*, published in 2009 is set against the backdrop of these events in Oakland and Berkeley. [159]

All of this was reflected in the lyrics of contemporary *folk* music. I find the music interesting and historical; but, alas, not a comforting sound or message. Forty years later, the songs remain troublesome to me.

THIRTY ONE: MARCHING BAND

I was never in a marching band because my high school's band became a causality of World War Two, when it was disbanded. No big loss for me because I was always on the field in a football uniform and too busy getting my head pushed into the turf to hear any band music -- that is, if we even had a band, or if I even played a band instrument. However, all of Aurdery and our four Keating children were in the marching band of Sylvania High School (Ohio) where Treci played the flute, Roger the trumpet, Lorie the clarinet, and Deke played Roger's hand-me-down coronet.

Marching bands perform a unique function in the American family culture: teenager-parent engagement. When a youngster moves into the difficult teenage years, their participation in the marching band becomes a defining activity that fills their boring days with activity and becomes a conversational grounding between parent and teenager.

> *"Dad, you can't believe what happened in band today during the rehearsal for Saturday's game. We were doing the half-time drill and Jack turned the wrong way and crashed headlong into me with his tuba. It was so funny!"*

A Marching Band is an activity in which musicians incorporate marching with their performance. Most bands use some kind of uniform that include the school's name and symbol. When Edgemont high school finally re-started their band at the end of the war, their uniforms were orange and black, the school colors.

I love watching a parade with band music and never miss our annual Sonora Mother-lode parade. Our local Sonora High school has a spectacular band of over 150 members -- it includes thirty percent of the student body and band is considered a "status" activity. My heart always skips a beat when the band goes marching past in their beautiful uniforms to the cadence of the drums.

Marching bands originated with travelling musicians who performed at festivals throughout the ancient world. It became structured within the armies of the early city-states, from which the modern marching band emerged. As musicians became less important in directing the movement of troops on the battlefield, the bands moved into increasingly ceremonial roles. Many military traditions still survive in the modern marching band. Bands will often be ordered to "*dress their ranks*" and "*cover down their files*". They may be called to "*attention*", and given orders such as "*about face*" and "*forward march*" (often done with whistles, hand signals, or baton.) Uniforms of many marching bands still resemble military uniforms.

Modern marching bands are commonly associated with football. In 1907, the first formation on a football field was by the Purdue All-American Marching Band. The first halftime show by a marching band was also in 1907 at a football game by the University of Illinois Marching Illini at a game against the University of Chicago. [160]

Another innovation that appeared at roughly the same time was the fight song. Many of the popular fight songs are widely utilized by high schools across the country. Four university fight songs commonly used are the University of Illinois' *Illinois Loyalty* (The school song for Edgemont High School); the University of Michigan's *The Victors* (The school song for Hot Springs -- our arch rivals); the University of Notre Dame's *Victory March* (son Roger was a member of their band); and the United States Naval Academy's *Anchors Aweigh*. [161]

A marching band is typically led by a drum major. A band requires leadership from within as well as from the drum major. Section leaders are selected from among the members of each instrumental section and are selected by the band director for their leadership skills. The section leader is as important a status role in high school as the various positions on the football squad -- I know this from the experience of my own children in high school. Lorie's position as section leader for clarinets was as important to her as Roger's position of 1st-string right-end on the football squad, and they both earned athletic "letters", school symbols which they proudly wore on their school jacket.

Bands have a repertoire of "traditional" music associated with their performances. The band of our local high school in Sonora has excellent musicians and is able to perform all the traditional band songs plus also popular music and the latest "show tunes". The Edgemont High School Marching Band with marginal musicians played only the simplest basics during the years they were re-starting. They sounded somewhat like the beginner band in the movie, *The Music Man*, who learned to play their instruments using the "think" method.

A name any band member will know is that of John Philip Sousa. He was and composer and conductor known for military and patriotic marches. He was born in Washington, D.C. in 1854 (during the Civil War), and died at the age of 78 in 1932. Sousa's father was a trombonist in the U.S. Marine band, and Sousa also served in the Marines. His most famous marches are *The Washington Post*, *Semper Fidelis* (Official March of the United States Marine Corps), and *The Stars and Stripes Forever*. (When I was in the third grade in Buffalo Gap, I was the Drum Major of our Rhythm Band, and we performed this song on the steps of the South Dakota State Capital in Pierre.)

John Philip Souza was the composer of much of the traditional band music still played today. He wrote 136 marches beginning in 1917. Some of his most popular and notable are: [162]

> *Semper Fidelity (1888) (Official March of the Marine Corps)*
>
> The Washington Post *(1889)*
>
> High School Cadets *(1890)*
>
> The Liberty Bell *(1893)*
>
> Manhattan Beach March *(1893)*

King Cotton *(1895)*

Stars and Stripes Forever *(1896) (National March of the U.S.)*

El Capitan *(1896)*

Hands Across the Sea (1899)

Hail to the Spirit of Liberty March (1900)

Invincible Eagle (1901)

U.S. Field Artillery *(1917) (Modified version* The Army Goes Rolling Along *is the official song of the* U.S. Army)

Who's Who in Navy Blue (1920)

The Black Horse Troop (1924)

Pride of the Wolverines (1926)

Minnesota March *(1927)*

New Mexico March (1928)

Salvation Army March (1930) (dedicated to The Salvation Army's 50th anniversary).

I am sure that anyone in a marching band played several of these marches. Sousa wrote marches for several American universities, including University of Illinois, University of Nebraska, Kansas State University, Marquette University, and University of Minnesota. What would a Saturday football afternoon be like without his music!

THIRTY TWO: ROCK'N'ROLL

Rock'n'roll is a style of popular music that originated in the 1950's, commonly also known as *rock*. It is heavily influenced by *rhythm & blues* and *country* and incorporated influences from *jazz* and *classical*. The sound is traditionally centered on the electric guitar, which is typically supported by the bass guitar and percussion that combines drums and cymbals, and is often accompanied by synthesizers. A group of musicians is termed a rock band and typically consists of between two and five members. [163]

Typically, *rock* is music with a 4/4 beat utilizing a verse-chorus form, but the genre has become extremely diverse. Lyrics often stress romantic love, but also a wide variety of other themes that are frequently social or political in emphasis. It places a higher degree of emphasis on musicianship, live performance, and an ideology of authenticity. [164]

By the late 1960's a number of sub-genres had emerged, including folk rock, blues-rock, and country rock, which contributed to the development of psychedelic rock influenced by the counter-cultural psychedelic (hippie) scene. New sub-genres that emerged included heavy metal (now called *hard rock*), which emphasized volume, power and speed. In the 1970's, punk rock reacted against the trends to produce a raw form of music characterized by overt political and social critiques. *Punk* was an influence into the 1980's with development of other sub-genres, including New Wave and eventually the alternative rock movement. *Rock* music has also served as the vehicle for social movements, including the "hippie" counterculture that spread out from San Francisco in the 1960's. Inheriting the *folk* tradition of the protest song, *rock* music has been associated with political activism as well as changes in social attitudes to race and sex. [165]

"*Rock* is traditionally built on a foundation of simple un-syncopated 4/4 rhythms, with a repetitive snare drum back beat. Harmonies range from the common triad to dissonant harmonic progressions. *Rock* songs often use the verse-chorus structure derived from *blues* and *folk* music. Critics have stressed the eclecticism and stylistic diversity of *rock*" [166] (Did you understand all that technical jargon of the trade? There will be a test later.)

There is debate about which should be considered the first rock'n'roll record. *Rock Around the Clock* (1955) became the first song to top Billboard charts, and opened the door worldwide for this new wave of popular culture. It has been argued that *That's All Right* (Mama) by Elvis Presley was the first *rock'n'roll* record, but Big Joe Turner's *Shake, Rattle, and Roll* was already at the top of the Billboard charts. Other artists with early *rock'n'roll* hits included Chuck Berry, Fats Domino, Little Richard, and Jerry Lee Lewis. Soon the style was the major force in American record sales. Crooners such as Eddie Fisher, Perry Como, and Patti Page, who had dominated the previous decade of popular music, found their access to the charts significantly curtailed. [167]

Elvis Presley was a towering figure in the *rock'n'roll* era. Rather than comment on his contributions here, I will refer you to the following chapter.

A decline of *rock'n'roll* occurred temporarily in the early 1960's due to a number of factors: the death of Buddy Holly in a plane crash, the departure of Elvis for the army, the retirement of Little Richard to become a preacher, prosecutions of Jerry Lee Lewis and Chuck Berry, and the payola scandal (which implicated major figures in bribery and corruption in promoting songs). The style gradually evolved. The advent of soul music was significant, led by pioneers like Ray Charles, James Brown, Aretha Franklin, and Stevie Wonder; and Motown became a major force in the record industry. These elements influenced the early work of The Beatles and through them the form of later *rock* music

Surf music achieved its greatest commercial success in the work of the Beach Boys, formed in 1961 in Southern California. Their early albums included instrumental *surf rock* and vocal songs, drawing on *rock'n'roll* and doo wop and the close harmonies of vocal pop acts like the Four Freshmen. Their first hit, *Surfin,* helped make the *surf* craze a national phenomenon. When Brian Wilson became their major composer and producer, the group moved on to more general themes of male adolescence including cars and girl in songs like Fun, Fun, Fun (1964) and California Girls (1965). Other *surf* acts followed, but only the *Beach Boys* were able to sustain a career into later years.

By the end of 1962, what would become the British rock "invasion" had started with groups like *The Beatles* and Rolling Stones. These groups composed their own material and infused it with a high energy beat. In 1964 the Beatles achieved a breakthrough to mainstream popularity in the United States. *I Want to Hold Your Hand* was the band's first hit. Their appearance on the Ed Sullivan Show is considered a milestone in American pop culture.

Today, *rock* music remains "alive and well," as evidenced by the fact that several winners of the popular TV show, *American Idol,* have been primarily *rock* performers.

THIRTY THREE: ELVIS PRESLEY

Elvis Presley was one of the most popular American singers of the 20th century. A cultural icon, he is widely known by the single name "Elvis". Presley's name and voice are instantly recognizable around the globe, and in polls he is recognized as one of the most important music artists and influential Americans. "*Elvis Presley is the greatest cultural force in the twentieth century*", said composer and conductor Leonard Bernstein.

> "*He introduced the beat to everything and he changed everything -- music, language, clothes. It's a whole new social revolution -- the sixties came from it.*" [168]

Born in Tupelo, Mississippi in 1935, Presley moved to Memphis with his family at the age of 13. His father moved from one odd job to the next, and the family often relied on help from neighbors and government food assistance. They lost their home after the father was found guilty of altering a check written by the landowner. He was jailed for eight months, and Elvis and his mother moved in with relatives and lived in poverty in public projects in neighborhoods that were mixed racially.

There was little in his early years to suggest the future career. He got "C" in music in the 8th grade. Presley, who never received formal music training or learned to read music, studied and played by ear. He was regarded as a loner, but began bringing his guitar to school on a daily basis. He would play and sing during lunchtime, and was often teased as a "trashy" kid who played "hillbilly" music. Once when he hosted a performance, Presley recalled that it did much for his reputation:

> *"I wasn't popular in school ... I failed music -- only thing I ever failed. And then they entered me in this talent show ... when I came onstage I heard people kind of rumbling and whispering and so forth, 'cause nobody knew I even sang. It was amazing how popular I became after that."* [169]

He began his career at the age of 19 when Sun Records, eager to bring the sound of African-American music to a wider audience, saw that his voice could be heard as either white with Black overtones, or visa versa. RCA Victor acquired his contract in a deal arranged by Colonel Tom Parker, who would manage the singer for over two decades. Parker was considered the best promoter in the music business. He brought Presley to national television, booking him on CBS's Stage Show for appearances over two months. The program was hosted by *Big Band* leaders and the brothers Tommy and Jimmy Dorsey. Presley's first RCA single, *Heartbreak Hotel,* released in January 1956, was a number one hit; that year he made his Hollywood film debut in *Love Me Tender.*

During a performance on the Steve Allen show, Presley abruptly halted a rendition of *Hound Dog* and launched into a slow, grinding version accentuated with energetic, exaggerated body movements. His gyrations created a storm of controversy. Television critics were outraged. Ben Gross of the New York Daily News said that popular music:

> *"has reached its lowest depths in the 'grunt and groin' antics of one Elvis Presley. ... Elvis, who rotates his pelvis ... gave an exhibition that was suggestive and vulgar, tinged with the kind of animalism that should be confined to dives and bordellos".* [170]

Ed Sullivan, whose variety show was the nation's most popular, declared him *"unfit for family viewing"*. To Presley's displeasure, he soon found himself being referred to as "Elvis the Pelvis", which he called *"one of the most childish expressions I ever heard, comin' from an adult."* He appeared on Steve Allen's show, which for the first time beat the CBS Ed Sullivan show in the ratings. Then Sullivan, despite his earlier pronouncement, booked the singer for three appearances for an unprecedented $50,000. The first, in September 1956, was seen by approximately 60 million viewers -- a record 82.6 percent of the television audience. More than any other single event, it was this first appearance on the Ed Sullivan Show that made Presley a national celebrity. [171]

Accompanying Presley's rise to fame, a cultural shift was taking place that he both helped inspire and came to symbolize, igniting; *"The biggest pop craze since* Glenn Miller *and* Frank Sinatra *... Presley brought rock'n'roll into the mainstream of popular culture. As Presley set the artistic pace, other artists followed. ... Presley, more than anyone else, gave the young a belief in themselves as a distinct and somehow unified generation -- the first in America ever to feel the power of an integrated youth culture."* [172]

His Hollywood films were almost universally panned; one critic dismissed them as a *"pantheon of bad taste".* Nonetheless, they were virtually all profitable. Hal Wallis, who produced nine of them, declared, *"A Presley picture is the only sure thing in Hollywood."*

This was still in the era of the universal draft in which all American men had to register and serve time in the military (unless they could find an exemption such as marriage or a temporary one to attend college). In 1958, Presley was drafted and inducted into the U.S. Army as a private at Fort Chaffee. The information officer said they were unprepared for the media attention drawn by the singer's arrival. Hundreds of people descended on Presley as he stepped from the bus. Presley announced that he was looking forward to his military stint, saying he did not want to be treated any differently from anyone else: *"The Army can do anything it wants with me."* After training at Fort Hood, Presley joined the 3rd Armored Division in Friedberg, Germany.

While in Germany, Presley met 14-year-old Priscilla Beaulieu. They would eventually marry after a seven-and-a-half-year courtship. In her autobiography, Priscilla says that despite his worries that it would ruin his career, Parker convinced Presley that to gain popular respect, he should serve his country as a regular soldier rather than in Special Services, where he would have been able to give some musical performances and remain in touch with the public.

Presley returned to the United States in 1960 and was honorably discharged with the rank of sergeant. The train that carried him to Tennessee was mobbed, and Presley was called upon to appear at scheduled stops to please his fans. Presley re-launched his recording career with some of his most commercially successful work. He proceeded to devote much of the 1960's to making Hollywood movies and soundtrack albums.

Shortly before Christmas 1966, more than seven years since they first met, Presley proposed to Priscilla Beaulieu. They were married in a brief ceremony in 1967 in their suite at the Aladdin Hotel in Las Vegas. Presley's only child, Lisa Marie, was born in 1968 during a period when he had grown deeply unhappy with his career. In an autobiography, Priscilla revealed that after her baby was born, Elvis virtually stopped having a sexual relationship with her. Presley and his wife became increasingly distant, barely cohabiting. Presley was rumored to have various affairs. The Presley's separated in 1972 after Priscilla disclosed her relationship with a karate instructor, and Presley and his wife filed for divorce.

Presley then had numerous girlfriends. He and Linda Thompson split, and he took up with a new girlfriend and gave her an engagement ring two months later. Reinforcing Presley's image as a sex symbol were the reports of his alleged dalliances with various Hollywood stars and starlets, from Natalie Wood in the 1950's to Connie Stevens and Ann-Margaret in the 1960's to Candice Bergen and Cybill Shepherd in the 1970's.

He was now becoming increasingly unwell. Twice during the following years he overdosed on barbiturates, spending three days in a coma in his hotel suite after the first incident. Toward the end of 1973, he was hospitalized, semi-comatose from the effects of Demerol addiction. It was obvious he was drugged. Hugely over-weight, his mind dulled by the pharmacopoeia, he was barely able to pull himself through his abbreviated concerts. In Louisiana, the singer was on stage for less than an hour; failed to appear in Baton Rouge; was unable to get out of his hotel bed; and the rest of the tour was cancelled. In Rapid City, South Dakota, he was so nervous on stage that he could hardly talk; unable to "perform any significant movement." [173]

Presley was scheduled to fly out of Memphis on the evening of August 16, 1977, to begin another tour. That afternoon, he was discovered unresponsive on his bathroom floor. Attempts to revive him failed, and death was officially pronounced at 3:30 pm at Baptist Memorial Hospital. Presley's funeral was held at Graceland, and 80,000 people lined the processional route to Forest Hill Cemetery, where Presley was buried next to his mother.

Graceland was opened to the public in 1982. Attracting over half a million visitors annually, it is the second most-visited home in the United States after the White House, and was declared a National Historic Landmark in 2006.

Presley is regarded as one of the most important figures of 20th-century popular culture. He had a versatile voice encompassing many genres, including *rock'n'roll, country,* pop, gospel, and blues. He is the best-selling solo artist in the history of popular music. Nominated for 14 Grammys, he won three, and received the Grammy Lifetime Achievement Award at age 36. Presley has been inducted into four music halls of fame: the Rock and Roll Hall of Fame (1986), the Country Music Hall of Fame (1998), the Gospel Music Hall of Fame (2001), and the Rockabilly Hall of Fame (2007).

The total number of his original master recordings has been variously calculated as 665 and 711. He was successful during an era when singles were the primary commercial medium for pop music.

Year	Singles [174]
1956	I Forgot to Remember to Forget
	Heartbreak Hotel
	I Want You, I Need You, I Love You
	Don't Be Cruel
	Hound Dog
	Love Me Tender
1957	Too Much
	All Shook Up
	(Let Me Be Your) Teddy Bear
	Jailhouse Rock
1958	Don't
	Hard Headed Woman
1959	One Night"/"I Got Stung
	A Fool Such as I / I Need Your Love Tonight"
	A Big Hunk o' Love
1960	Stuck on You
	It's Now or Never
	Are You Lonesome Tonight?
1961	Wooden Heart
	Surrender
	(Marie's the Name) His Latest Flame / Little Sister
1962	Can't Help Falling in Love"/"Rock-A-Hula Baby
	Good Luck Charm
	She's Not You
	Return to Sender
1963	(You're The) Devil in Disguise
1965	Crying in the Chapel
1969	Suspicious Minds
1970	The Wonder of You
1977	Moody Blue
	Way Down
1981	Guitar Man (reissue)
2002	A Little Less Conversation (JXL remix)

2005	*Jailhouse Rock (reissue)*	
	One Night / I Got Stung (reissue)	
	It's Now or Never (reissue)	

THIRTY FOUR: COUNTRY MUSIC

My 1950's era *Colliers Encyclopedia* did not have a single mention of *country music* in its index; that term had not yet been bestowed. Unlike some genres that suddenly burst forth, *country* matured slowly over nearly a century with style changes and name changes. Early roots can be traced to the 1920's when it was referred to as *"hillbilly"* (the name was later seen to be denigrating), then to *"country and western"*, and finally in the 1970's it became *country*. During those changes the artists changed from Jimmy Rogers (with his Hillbilly song *Blue Yodel*), to Gene Autry (*Back in the Saddle Again*), Eddie Arnold (*Make the World Go Away*), Ray Charles (*I can't stop loving you*), and Willie Nelson (*On the Road Again*). The locale also changed from Texas to Nashville.

Country music has produced the two top selling solo artists of all time: Elvis Presley and Garth Brooks. Elvis is the top solo artist in U.S. history, and Garth is the second best solo artist. [175]

Columbia Records began issuing records with *"hillbilly"* music as early as 1924 with Jimmie Rodgers and the Carter Family. Rodgers fused *hillbilly, country, gospel, jazz, blues, pop*, and *cowboy*. Many of his songs were his own compositions including *Blue Yodel*, which established Rodgers as the premier singer of early *country* music. The Carters recorded old-time ballads, *country* songs and Gospel hymns, all representatives of America's southeastern folklore where the genre took its roots. [176]

During the 1930's Great Depression, radio became popular and "barn dance" shows featuring country music were started all over the South. The Grand Ole Opry started earlier in 1925 in Nashville. Two of the early stars on the *Opry* were Roy Acuff and Minnie Pearl. During his career, Eddy Arnold placed 147 songs on the *country* music charts. (He is my favorite *country* singer and the reason I started listening to this genre of music. Prior to his time, it seemed to me that all *country* vocalists had an offensive twang to their voice and silly *hillbilly* lyrics. His brand of *country* was the first that appealed to me.) Apparently I was not alone in my tastes, because he became popular nationwide, starred in his own TV show, and is in the *Country Music Hall of Fame.* [177]

During the 1930's and 1940's, cowboy songs were popularized by Hollywood films. Singing cowboys included Gene Autry, Roy Rogers, Spade Cooley, Tex Williams, and Bob Wills; and cowgirls also contributed. Patsy Montana opened the door with her song *I Want to Be a Cowboy's Sweetheart.*

In 1938, Bob Wills was one of the first to add an electric guitar to his band. Nashville players preferred the warm tones of the Gibson and Gretsch electrics, but the "hot" Fender style that became available in the early 1950's, eventually prevailed as the signature guitar sound of *country.* [178]

Several sub-genres appeared during world War Two. "*Hillbilly boogie*" with Tennessee Ernie Ford lasted into the 1950's. String-band music known as "bluegrass" had emerged; introduced by Roy Acuff at the Grand Ole Opry. Red Foley had one of the first gospel hits *Peace in the Valley* and also sang *boogie, blues* and *rockabilly.* The Billboard replaced the term "*hillbilly*" with "*folk songs and blues*" and switched to "*country*" or "*country and Western*" in 1949. [179]

Another type of guitar music, "*honky tonk*", with roots in Texas became popular. This music has been described as:

> "A little bit of this, and a little bit of that,
> a little bit of black and a little bit of white...
> just loud enough to keep you from thinking too much,
> and to go right on ordering the whiskey."

Two of my favorites were *Honky Tonk Blues* and *Pistol Packin' Mama.*

They became popular when I was in college at fraternity-sorority "beer busts". Someone would start a bonfire, pull out a guitar, and a song fest would last until late into the night when the girls all had to quickly depart in time for dormitory curfew.

In the early 1950's a mixture of rock'n'roll and *hillbilly* called "*rockabilly*", became popular. During this period Elvis Presley converted over to *country* music. The number two, three and four songs on charts were Elvis Presley's, Heartbreak Hotel; Johnny Cash's, I Walk the Line; and Carl Perkin's, Blue Suede Shoes. Elvis acknowledged the influence of *rhythm and blues* in his style commenting: *"the colored folk been singin' and playin' it just the way I'm doin' it now, man for more years than I know."* But he also said, *"My stuff is just hopped-up country."* [180]

In the mid 1950's, the "Nashville sound" turned country music into a multimillion-dollar industry centered in Nashville. Roy Acuff organized the first publishing house for country music, and Hank Williams helped establish Nashville as the undisputed centre of country music along with other performers such as Tex Ritter, Johnny Cash, Loretta Lynn, Tammy Wynette, Buck Owens, Merle Haggard, Patsy Cline, Loretta Lynn, Reba McIntyre, Eddie Arnold, Charlie Rich, and Charley Pride. Ray Charles surprised the pop world by turning his attention to country and western music, topping the charts with I Can't Stop Loving You. [181]

Another sub-genre of country music originated in Bakersfield, California, and grew out of *honky tonk* with elements of swing. It relied in particular on the electric guitar and had a sharp, hard, driving, no-frills, edgy flavor. Leading practitioners of this "*Bakersfield*" style were Buck Owens and Merle Haggard.

In the decades that followed, artists such as Juice Newton, Alabama, Hank Williams, Jr., Shania Twain, Brooks & Dunn, Faith Hill, Garth Brooks, Dwight Yoakam, Dolly Parton, Rosanne Cash and Linda Ronstadt moved country further towards *rock* influence.

A sub-genre called "*outlaw*" country was derived from the anger of an alienated sub-culture during the 1960's. It is associated with Hank Williams, Jr, Willie Nelson, and Waylon Jennings. Nelson was one of the main figures of *outlaw country* and has acted in over 30 films, coauthored several books and has been involved with several causes. [182] Asked about *outlaw country*, he remarked:

> " *After I left Nashville, I wanted to relax and play the music that I wanted to play, and just stay around Texas, maybe Oklahoma. Waylon and I had that outlaw image going, and when it caught on at colleges and we started selling records, we were O.K. The whole outlaw thing -- it had nothing to do with the music -- it was something that got written in an article, and the young people said, 'Well, that's pretty cool.' And started listening.*" [183]

A sub-genre that first emerged in the 1970's is *country pop*. It started with singers like Glen Campbell, John Denver, Olivia Newton-John, Marie Osmond, B. J. Thomas and Anne Murray having hits on the *country* charts. Campbell's *Rhinestone Cowboy* was one of the biggest crossover hits. In 1974, Newton-John an Australian pop singer, won the "Best Female Country Vocal Performance" as well as the Country Music Association's most coveted award, "Female Vocalist of the Year".

Dolly Parton, already a successful *country* artist, crossed over to *pop* music with her hit *Here You Come Again*. Coming from the other direction, Kenny Rogers aimed his music at the *country* charts after a successful career in *pop*, achieving success with *Lucille*. Parton and Rogers would continue to have success on both *country* and *pop* charts; and singers like Reba McIntyre, Crystal Gayle, Ronnie Milsap and Barbara Mandrell would find success on both the *pop* and *country* charts with their records as well.

During the early 1980's, *country* artists continued to see their *pop* records perform well. Willie Nelson charted *Always On My Mind* and *To All The Girls I've Loved Before*, while Juice Newton achieved success with *Queen of Hearts* and *Angel of the Morning*. A crossover hit was written by Barry, Robin, and Maurice Gibb of the Bee Gees. *Endless Love* by Diana Ross and Lionel Richie, and Roy Orbison's *You Got It* were hits. The group, *Alabama*, was named Artist of the Decade for the 1980's by the Academy of Country Music. A group of new artists began to emerge led by Randy Travis and included Travis Tritt, Ricky Skaggs, Kathy Mattea, George Strait, Clint Black, and the Judds.

In the mid 1990's, *country* music was influenced by the popularity of line dancing. This influence was so great that Chet Atkins was quoted as saying *"The music has gotten pretty bad, I think. It's all that damn line dancing."* By the end of the decade, however, at least one line dance choreographer complained that good *country* line dance music was no longer being released. (My wife, Aurdery, and I had recently moved to a ranch in cowboy country near Sonora in the Sierra Mountain foothills. We joined a country music class being taught at the local community college, and I purchased cowboy boots and a Stetson hat to help me look the part.

Taylor Swift rose as a *country-pop* artist with her Love Story and You Belong with Me. Both became the best-selling *country* songs of all time. Swift's Fearless was awarded the Grammy for "Album of the Year", also winning the American Music Award, Academy of Country Music Award, and *Country Music Association Award.*

In 2009, George Strait was named "Artist of the Decade" by the *Academy of Country Music.* It was apparent that the long climb from the 1920s for *country* music had been successfully accomplished.

The performers we have discussed, for the most part, were stars during the past decade or before, but we are already into the second decade of the 21st century. In looking at *"Music: Then and Now"*, let's consider the *"Now"*. Who are singers of this new generation who seem destined to become superstars during this decade and beyond? Carrie Underwood recently rose to fame with her first single, Inside Your Heaven, and she became the only *country* artist to have a #1 hit on the Billboard chart in this decade. She is already a multi-platinum recording artist. There is more on this rising superstar in a following chapter.

The following is a list of better known *country* singers.

COUNTRY SINGERS

Roy Acuff	Alabama	Allman Brothers
Lynn Anderson	Eddy Arnold	Chet Atkins

Gene Autry	Clint Black	Lisa Hartman Black
Garth Brooks	Brooks & Dunn	Jimmy Buffett
Glen Campbell	Mary Chapin Carpenter	Johnny Cash
June Carter Cash	Ray Charles	Kenny Chesney
Roy Clark	Patsy Cline	Rita Coolidge
Kevin Costner	Sheryl Crow	Billy Ray Cyrus
Charlie Daniels	Jimmy Dean	John Denver
Dixie Chicks	Clint Eastwood	Dale Evans
Everly Brothers	Freddy Fender	Tennessee Ernie Ford
Larry Gatlin	Crystal Gayle	Vince Gill
Lee Greenwood	Woody Guthrie	Merle Haggard
Faith Hill	Julianne Hough	Burl Ives
Alan Jackson	Waylon Jennings	Jewel
George Jones	Kris Kristofferson	Lady Antebellum
Miranda Lambert	k.d. lang	Brenda Lee
Jerry Lee Lewis	Patty Loveless	Lyle Lovett
Loretta Lynn	Barbara Mandrell	Dean Martin
Martina McBride	Reba McEntire	Tim McGraw
Roger Miller	Ronnie Milsap	Anne Murray
Willie Nelson	Aaron Neville	Olivia Newton-John
Oak Ridge Boys	Marie Osmond	Buck Owens
Patti Page	Brad Paisley	Dolly Parton
Johnny Paycheck	Minnie Pearl	Elvis Presley
Charley Pride	Eddie Rabbitt	Bonnie Raitt
Charlie Rich	Leann Rimes	Tex Ritter
Roy Rogers	Linda Ronstadt	Shenandoah
Ricky Skaggs	Sons of the Pioneers	Statler Brothers
George Strait	Taylor Swift	Mel Tillis
Randy Travis	Travis Tritt	Tanya Tucker
Shania Twain	Conway Twitty	Carrie Underwood
Keith Urban	Hank Williams	Hank Williams, Jr.
Tex Williams	Lee Ann Womack	Tammy Wynette
Wynonna	Trisha Yearwood	Smiley Burnette
Emmylou Harris	Roy Orbison	Rosanne Cash

THIRTY FIVE: CARRY UNDERWOOD

Carrie Underwood is already a superstar and is destined for a soaring career in the years to come. Born in 1983, she is a singer, songwriter, and actress who rose to fame as winner of the fourth season of American Idol. Underwood has since become a multi-platinum recording artist, a multiple Grammy Award winner, a member of the Grand Ole Opry, a Golden Globe Award nominee, a three-time Academy of Country Music and Country Music Association Female Vocalist winner, a GMA Dove award winner, and a two-time ACM Entertainer of the Year. She is the first-ever female artist to win back-to-back Academy of Country Music (ACM) Awards for Entertainer of the Year (2009/10). [184]

Underwood was born to Stephen and Carole Underwood in Muskogee, Oklahoma, and was raised on her parents' farm in the rural town of Checotah, Oklahoma. Her father worked in sawmills and her mother taught elementary school. During her childhood, Underwood performed at talent shows and sang at the Baptist Church. She later sang for local events, including Old Settler's Day and the Lion's Club. Underwood is an enrolled member of the Muscogee (Creek) Nation.

After high school, she attended Northeastern State University in Tahlequah, Oklahoma, graduating magna cum laude with a bachelor's degree in mass communication and journalism. Underwood is an alumna of the of Sigma Sigma Sigma sorority, and competed in numerous beauty pageants at the university. In the summer of 2004, Underwood auditioned for American Idol. After she sang *Could've Been*, judge Simon

Cowell commented that she would be one of the favorites. During the final episode, Underwood sang the *rock* hit *Alone*, and after performing *Angels Brought me Here*, Cowell said that she had done enough to win and would outsell all previous winners. One of the show's producers later said she dominated the voting, winning each week handily. [185]

Underwood came back to perform on American Idol each of the following four seasons with her singles: *Jesus Take the Wheel*; *Wasted*; *Go Your Own Way*, and *I Told You So* (in a duet with Randy Travis); and on season nine sang *Undo It*, and *Together We Are One* with previous Idol winners as a farewell to Simon Cowell.

Underwood performed at the 40th Annual Country Music Association Awards in 2006, and won both the Horizon Award for new country artists and Female Vocalist -- the first time since 1995 that an artist won both Awards. That year Underwood also performed for U.S. Army Troops on a USO tour in Iraq

Madame Tussaud's unveiled Underwood's wax figure on Times Square, New York City, in 2008. The general manager commented:

> *"We are thrilled that Carrie was able to join us today to help unveil her figure. Not only is she a bona fide superstar with fans around the world, but she is also an incredibly kind and generous young woman -- a true role model for young people today. We know that our guests will love her figure, and we can't wait for them to see it."* [186]

In 2009, Underwood won the prestigious trophy for Entertainer of The Year. Previous female winners include Loretta Lynn in 1975, Dolly Parton in 1977, Barbara Mandrell in 1980, Reba McEntire in 1994, Shania Twain in 1999, and most recently Dixie Chicks in 2000.

In May 2010, Underwood was selected on People Magazine's Most Beautiful People List for 2010, the 4th year in a row that she was selected for this prestigious list. On 2011, Underwood made her Hollywood screen debut in Soul Surfer.

Where Carry Underwood goes on from here is difficult to predict, but she is likely to soar even higher.

THIRTY SIX: MUSICAL THEATRE

Many of our popular songs first appeared in Broadway musicals or in Hollywood films. Musical theatre combines songs, dialogue, and dance, and the emotional content -- humor, pathos, love, and anger -- is created with music and action. Musicals are performed all around the world and may be on Broadway or in Off-Broadway productions, on tour, in local theatres, or in schools.

Although music has been a part of theatre since ancient times, modern musicals emerged during the 19th century with the operettas of Gilbert and Sullivan, followed by creators like George M. Cohan. Early in the 20th century, musicals led to modern classics such as *Show Boat* and *Oklahoma!* Others that followed have included *West Side Story, The Fantasticks, Hair, Chorus Line, Les Misérables, The Phantom of the Opera, Rent, The Producers* and *My Fair Lady*.

The material in a musical may be original or it may be adapted from novels (*Wicked* and *Man of La Mancha*), or from plays (*Hello, Dolly!*), classic legends (*Camelot*), historical events (*Evita*), or from films (*The Producers* and *Hairspray*). On the other hand, many musicals have later been adapted for films, such as *The Sound of Music, West Side Story, My Fair Lady*, and *Chicago*.

A musical's moments of greatest dramatic intensity are often performed in song.

> *"When the emotion becomes too strong for speech you sing; when it becomes too strong for song, you dance."* [187]

Closely related to musical theatre is opera. Works by George Gershwin, Leonard Bernstein and Stephen Sondheim have received both musical theatre and operatic productions.

The 20th century brought a profusion of musicals by Jerome Kern and other Tin Pan Alley composers with musical styles such as ragtime and jazz. Then came shows like *Lady be good, No, No, Nanette,* and *Funny Face.* While the story lines of these shows may have been forgettable, they produced dozens of enduring popular songs by Cole Porter, George and Ira Gershwin, Irving Berlin, Rodgers and Hart, and featured stars such as Ginger Rogers and Fred Astaire.

Rising above the musicals of the decade, *Show Boat,* which premiered in 1927 on Broadway, was told through music, dialogue, setting and movement, woven together seamlessly (Music by Kern, lyrics by Hammerstein). It was the first musical to provide a cohesive plot and the use of music that was integral to the narrative. Based on a novel by Edna Ferber, the musical presented a drama incorporating music that was derived from American *folk* melodies. [188]

Rodgers and Hammerstein's *Oklahoma* completed the revolution begun by Show Boat, by tightly integrating all the aspects of musical theatre with a cohesive plot, songs that furthered the action of the story, featured dream ballets that advanced the plot, and developed the characters. The two collaborators, Rodgers and Hammerstein, created an extraordinary collection of some of musical theatre's most enduring classics, including *Carousel, South Pacific, The King and I,* and *The Sound of Music.* These shows ushered in the "Golden Age" of American musical theatre. [189]

In the 1930s, Rodgers & Hart churned out a series of lighthearted Broadway hits including *On Your Toes, Babes In Arms, I'd Rather Be Right,* and *The Boys From Syracuse.* Cole Porter wrote a similar string of hits, including *Anything Goes, Can-Can* and *Silk Stockings.* The 1940's would begin with more hits from Porter, Irving Berlin, Rodgers and Hart, Weill and Gershwin.

Damon Runyon's eclectic characters were at the core of *Guys and Dolls* and the California gold rush was the setting for Lerner and Loews's *Paint Your Wagon* (1951). Lerner and Loewe collaborated again on *My Fair Lady* (1956), an adaptation of George Bernard Shaw's *Pygmalion* starring Rex Harrison and Julie Andrews. Popular Hollywood movies were made of all of these musicals. [190]

Dance was an integral part of *West Side Story* (1957), which transported *Romeo and Juliet* to modern day New York City and converted the feuding Montague and Capulet families into opposing ethnic gangs, the Jets and the Sharks. The book was adapted by Arthur Laurents, with music by Leonard Bernstein and lyrics by newcomer Stephen Sondheim. It was embraced by the critics but failed to be a popular choice for theatre goers who preferred Meredith Wilson's small town of River City in *The Music Man* to the alleys of Manhattan's Upper West Side. Apparently Tony Award voters were of a similar mind. *West Side Story* had a respectable run, but *The Music Man* ran nearly twice as long.

Laurents and Sondheim teamed up again for *Gypsy* (1959), providing the music for a story about stripper Gypsy Rose Lee. Ethel Merman made the role famous and it was given four revivals with Angela Lansbury, Tyne Daly, Bernadette Peters and Patti LuPone later tackling the role. The 1950's ended with Rodgers and Hammerstein's *The Sound of Music*, starring Mary Martin. With its successful 1965 film version, it has become one of the most popular musicals in history. [191]

In 1960, *The Fantasticks* was produced off-Broadway. This allegorical show would run for over 40 years at the Sullivan Street Theatre in Greenwich Village, becoming the longest-running musical in history. The 1960's decade would see a number of blockbusters like *Fiddler on the Roof* (1964), *Hello, Dolly!* (1964), *Funny Girl* (1964), *Man of La Mancha* (1965), and some risqué pieces like *Cabaret*.

Sondheim wrote both music and lyrics for *A Funny Thing Happened on the Way to the Forum* (1962). Other Sondheim works include *Anyone Can Whistle* (1964), *Company* (1970), *Follies* (1971), *A Little Night Music* (1973), *Pacific Overtures* (1976), *Sweeney Todd* (1979), and *Assassins* (1990). While some critics have argued that Sondheim's musicals lack commercial appeal, others have praised their musical complexity, as well as the interplay of lyrics and music in his shows.

Jerry Herman played a significant role in American musical theatre, beginning with his first Broadway production, *Milk and Honey* (1961), and continuing with the smash hits *Hello, Dolly!* (1964), *Mame* (1966), and *La Cage aux Folles* (1983). Writing both words and music, many of Herman's show tunes have become popular standards, including *Hello, Dolly!, We Need a Little Christmas, I Am What I Am, Mame, The Best of Times, Before the Parade Passes By, Put On Your Sunday Clothes, It Only Takes a Moment, Bosom Buddies,* and *I Won't Send Roses*. Some recorded by such artists as Louis Armstrong, Eydie Gorme, Barbra Streisand, Petula Clark and Bernadette Peter.

Chorus Line first opened at a public theater in lower Manhattan with music by Marvin Hamlisch and lyrics by Edward Kleban. Advance word-of-mouth -- that something extraordinary was about to explode -- boosted box office sales, and after critics ran out of superlatives to describe what they witnessed on opening night, what initially had been planned as a limited engagement eventually moved to Broadway, becoming the longest-running production in Broadway history up to that time. The show swept the Tony Awards and won the Pulitzer Prize, and its hit song, *What I Did for Love*, became an instant standard.

Broadway audiences welcomed musicals that varied from the usual style and substance. At the end of the decade, *Evita* gave a more serious political biography than audiences were used to. *Sweeney Todd* was the precursor to the darker, big budget musicals of the 1980's that depended on dramatic stories, sweeping scores and spectacular effects like *Les Misérables, Miss Saigon,* and *The Phantom of the Opera*. But during this same period, old-fashioned values were still embraced in such hits as *Annie, 42nd Street, My One and Only,* and popular revivals of *No, No, Nanette* and *Irene*.

In recent years, familiarity has been embraced by producers and investors anxious to guarantee that they recoup their considerable investments, if not show a healthy profit. Some took chances on the new and unusual, such as *The 25th Annual Putnam County Spelling Bee* (2005), but most took a safe route with revivals of familiar fare, such as *Fiddler on the Roof, A Chorus Line, South Pacific, Gypsy, Hair, West Side Story* and *Grease*, or with other proven material from films: *The Producers, Spamalot, Hairspray, The Color Purple, Xanadu,* and *Shrek.* [192]

After the 1996 Hollywood film of *Evita*, Baz Luhrmann continued with the film musical *Moulin Rouge!* (2001). This was followed by a series of film musicals, including *Chicago* (2002); *Phantom of the Opera* (2004); *Dreamgirls* (2006); *Hairspray, Across the Universe, Enchanted* and *Sweeney Todd* (2007); *Mamma Mia!* (2008); and *Nine* (2009). Dr. Seuss's *How the Grinch Stole Christmas!* (2000) and *The Cat in the Hat* (2003), turned children's books into live-action movie musicals. After the success of Disney with animated film beginning with *The Little Mermaid* in 1989, other animated movie musicals were released in the first decade of the 21st century.

Musicals made for television became popular in the 1990's, such as *Gypsy* (1993), *Cinderella* (1997) and *Annie* (1999). Several TV musicals in the 21st century were adaptations of a stage version, such as *South Pacific* (2001), *The Music Man* (2003),*Once Upon A Mattress* (2005), and *Legally Blonde* (2007). Additionally, several musicals were filmed on stage and later broadcast on Public Television, for example *Contact* (2002), *Kiss Me Kate* and *Oklahoma!* (2003).

All this prompts one to ask the question: "Is musical theatre dead? ...Absolutely not! Changing? Always! The musical has been changing ever since it first appeared over a century ago; and this is the clearest sign that the musical is still a living, growing genre. Will we ever return to the so-called "golden age", with musicals at the center of popular culture? Maybe! Public taste continues to change, and the commercial arts can only flow where the paying public spends its money. [193]

The following is a list of the 100 longest running musicals.

LONGEST RUNNING MUSICALS

1. PHANTOM OF THE OPERA
2. CATS
3. LES MISERABLES
4. A CHORUS LINE
5. CHICAGO

6. OH! CALCUTTA!
7. THE LION KING
8. BEAUTY AND THE BEAST
9. RENT
10. MISS SAIGON
11. MAMMA MIA!
12. 42nd STREET
13. GREASE
14. FIDDLER ON THE ROOF
15. LIFE WITH FATHER
16. TOBACCO ROAD
17. WICKED
18. HELLO, DOLLY!
19. MY FAIR LADY
20. HAIRSPRAY
21. AVENUE Q
22. THE PRODUCERS
23. (tied) CABARET
24. (tied) ANNIE
25. MAN OF La MANCHA
26. ABIE"S IRISH ROSE
27. JERSEYH BOYS
28. OKLAHOMA!
29. SMOKEY JOE'S CAFÉ
30. PIPPIN
31. SOUTH PACIFIC
32. THE MAGIC SHOW
33. MARY POPPINS
34. AIDA
35. GEMINI
36. DEATHTRAP
37. HARVEY
38. DANCIN'
39. La CAGE AUX FOLLES
40. HAIR

41. THE WIZ
42. BORN YESTERDAY
43. CRAZY FOR YOU
44. AIN'T MISBEHAVIN'
45. THE LITTLE BEST WHOREHOUSE IN TEXAS
46. SPAMALOT
47. MARY, MARY
48. EVITA
49. THE VOICE OF THE TURTLE
50. JEKYLL & HYDE
51. BAREFOOT IN THE PARK
52. 42nd STREET
53. DREAMGIRLS
54. MAME
55. GREASE
56. SAME TIME NEXT YEAR
57. ARSENIC AND OLD LACE
58. THE SOUND OF MUSIC
59. ME AND MY GIRL
60. HOW TO SUCCEED IN BUSINESS WITHOUT REALLY TRYING
61. HELLZAPOPPIN'
62. THE MUSIC MAN
63. FUNNY GIRL
64. MUMMENSCHANZ
65. OH! CALCUTTA!
66. MOVIN' OUT
67. BRIGHTON BEACH
68. ANGEL STREET (Also known as GAS LIGHT)
69. LIGHTNIN'
70. PROMISES. PROMISES
71. THE KING AND I
72. CACTUS FLOWER
73. (tied) SLEUTH
74. (tied) TORCH SONG TRILOGY

75. 1776
76. EQUUS
77. SUGAR BABIES
78. GUYS AND DOLLS
79. IN THE HEIGHTS
80. AMADEUS
81. CABARET
82. MISTER ROBERTS
83. ANNIE GET YOUR GUN
84. GUYS AND DOLLS
85. THE SEVEN YEAR ITCH
86. THE 25th ANNUAL PUTNAM COUNTY SPELLING BEE
87. BRING IN 'DA NOISE, BRING IN 'DA FUNK
88. BUTTERFLIES ARE FREE
89. PINS AND NEEDLES
90. PLAZA SUITE
91. FOSSE
92. THEY'RE PLAYING OUR SONG
93. KISS ME, KATE
94. DON'T BOTHER ME, I CAN'T COPE
95. THE PAJAMA GAME
96. BILLY ELLIOT THE MUSICAL
97. SHENANDOAH
98. ANNIE GET YOUR GUN
99. THE TEAHOUSE OF THE AUGUST MOON
100. DAMN YANKEES

THIRTY SEVEN: JACKIE EVANCHO

A look to the future of music should focus on young talents such as Jacqueline "Jackie" Evancho, not yet a teenager. Born in 2000, she is well on her way to becoming a superstar. Jackie was "discovered" after performing on the TV show, *America's Got Talent*. With the release of her *O Holy Night*, she became the best-selling debut artist of 2010 and again the following year with *Dream with Me*. In addition to performing vocal music, Evancho plays the violin and piano, and writes song lyrics. [194]

Evancho was born to Michael and Lisa Evancho and has two brothers and a sister. She resides in a suburb of Pittsburgh. She started singing when watching the musical *The Phantom of the Opera*; her mother heard her singing and allowed her to enter a local talent contest at age 8. She sang *Wishing You Were Somehow Here Again*, finishing as first runner-up, and began taking vocal lessons after the contest.

In 2009, Evancho released her debut album called *Prelude to a Dream*. The album featured songs: Andrea Bocelli's *Con te partirò* and *The Prayer*; Josh Groban's *To Where You Are*; Martina McBride's *Concrete Angel*; and a rendition of *Amazing Grace*.

Evancho was a contestant on the fifth season of the America's Got Talent TV show and performed *O mio babbino caro* by Giacomo Puccini. She received a standing ovation after her performance.

Her semifinal performance was *Time To Say Goodbye*. She advanced to the Top 10, where she performed *Pie Jesu* by Andrew Lloyd Webber.

Her final competition performance was *Ave Maria*. On the season finale, she performed *Time To Say Goodbye* with Sarah Brightman.

Evancho's first release on a major record label was a Columbia Records EP entitled *O Holy Night*. It reached #1 on Amazon's bestsellers in music. Evancho also debuted at #1 on Billboard's Classical Albums Chart. The album was certified platinum. [195]

Christopher Hahn, General Director of the Pittsburgh Opera said Evancho's performance of *O mio babbino caro* was spellbinding.

> *"It's very unusual for a young child to have a voice that sounded so rich and developed. I thought she was just lovely, sweetly compelling. It is quite unusual to hear a young girl with that level of warmth and roundness. Her phrasing was lovely, which she needed for that piece."* [196]

America's Got Talent judge Piers Morgan said that Evancho has more talent than any act he has seen after witnessing her version of *Ave Maria*:

> *"I have never seen an act, on this show or the British show or any of the other talent shows in the world, with more potential than Jackie Evancho. That was perfection. Perfection!"* [197]

Already a superstar at age eleven, where does she go from here?

THIRTY EIGHT: OPERA

When I was in graduate school at U.C. Berkeley, I had season tickets to the opera. Attending a Puccini opera in the San Francisco Opera House is an elegant and enjoyable evening.

Opera is a forerunner to musical theatre and part of our Western musical tradition. It combines text, a musical score, and incorporates many of the elements of theatre such as acting, scenery, costumes, and sometimes even includes dance. The performance is typically given in an opera house, accompanied by an orchestra.

Opera started in Italy at the end of the 16th century and soon spread through the rest of Europe. The word *opera* means "work" in Italian. It combines the arts of singing, declamation, acting and dancing in a staged spectacle.

The most renowned figure of 18th century opera is Mozart, who is famous for his Italian comic operas, especially *The Marriage of Figaro,* Don Giovanni, and *Così fan tutte.* The 19th century was a "golden age" of opera, dominated by Wagner, Verdi, Rossini, Donizetti and Bellini. The popularity of opera continued with Puccini and Strauss in the early 20th century.

In the 19th century, Giuseppe Verdi's operas resonated with the growing spirit of Italian nationalism in the post-Napoleonic era, and he quickly became an icon of the patriotic movement. In the 1850's, Verdi produced his three most popular operas: *Rigoletto, Il trovatore* and *La traviata.* He continued to develop his style, composing perhaps the greatest French Grand Opera, *Don Carlos*, and ending his career with two Shakespeare-inspired works, *Otello* and *Falstaff*, which reveal how far Italian opera had grown in sophistication since the early 19th century.

The sentimental "realistic" melodrama then appeared in Italy. This was a style introduced by Pietro Mascagni's *Cavalleria Rusticana*. Ruggero Leoncavallo's *Pagliacci* came to dominate the world's opera stages along with such popular works as Giacomo Puccini's *La bohème*, *Tosca*, and *Madama Butterfly*.

Wagner was a revolutionary composer. In his music dramas, *Tristan und Isolde, Die Meistersinger von Nürnberg, Der Ring des Nibelungen* and *Parsifal*, he avoided the distinction between aria and recitative in favor of a seamless flow of "endless melody".

Richard Strauss accepted Wagnerian ideas but took them in wholly new directions. He first won fame with the scandalous *Salome* and the dark tragedy *Elektra*; then Strauss changed tack in his greatest success, *Der Rosenkavalier*. Strauss continued to produce a highly varied body of operatic works until *Capriccio* in 1942. In the second half of the 19th century, Jacques Offenbach created operetta with witty and cynical works such as *Orphée aux enfers*, as well as the opera *Les Contes d'Hoffmann*. Charles Gounod scored a massive success with *Faust*. Bizet composed *Carmen*, which became the most popular of all opera, once audiences learned to accept its blend of Romanticism and realism.

By the 1930's, some musicals began to be written with an operatic structure. These include *Porgy and Bess* (1935) influenced by jazz styles, and *Candide* (1956) with its farcical parodies of opera. Telling dramatic stories through complex music and now sometimes seen in opera houses are: *Show Boat, West Side Story, Brigadoon, Sweeney Todd, Evita, The Light in the Piazza,* and *The Phantom of the Opera*. Some musicals, beginning with *Tommy* (1969) and *Jesus Christ Superstar* (1971) and continuing through *Les Misérables* (1980), *Rent* (1996) and *Spring Awakening* (2006), use various operatic conventions, and tell dramatic stories predominantly through rock, pop or contemporary music.

A common trend throughout the 20th century is the use of smaller orchestras as a cost-cutting measure. The grand Romantic-era orchestras with huge string sections, multiple harps, extra horns, and exotic percussion instruments were no longer feasible. As government and private patronage of the arts decreased throughout the 20th century, new works were often commissioned and performed with smaller budgets. Another feature is the emergence of contemporary historical operas; examples are: *The Death of Klinghoffer, Nixon in China, Doctor Atomic bomb,* and *Dead Man Walking.*

The Metropolitan Opera in the US reports that the average age of its audience is now 60, and opera companies are attempting to attract a younger audience. This is part of the larger trend of graying audiences for classical music. In an effort to attract younger audiences, the Metropolitan Opera offers a student discount on ticket purchases. Smaller opera companies have a more fragile existence and they usually depend on support from state and local governments, local businesses, and fundraisers. In addition to radio and television broadcasts of opera performances, which have had some success in gaining new audiences, broadcasts of performances in movie theatres have shown the potential to reach new audiences. Since 2006, the Met has broadcast live performances to several hundred movie screens all over the world.

Major opera houses have begun broadcasting their performances to local cinemas throughout the United States and in many other countries. The Metropolitan Opera began high-definition television transmissions in 2006. In 2007, Met performances were shown in over 424 theaters in U.S. cities. La bohème went out to 671 screens worldwide. San Francisco Opera began prerecorded broadcasts in March 2008. European opera houses such as La Scala in Milan, the Salzburg Festival, La Fenice in Venice and the Maggio Musicale in Florence have also broadcast their productions to theaters in ninety cities since 2006. The Internet is also affecting the way in which audiences consume opera. In 2009 British Opera house, Glyndebourne, made available online a full digital video download of Wagner's *Tristan und Isolde.*

So like all other forms of communication, the centuries -old music of opera is now adapting to the venues of the modern age.

THIRTY NINE: THE DOWN-SIDE OF "GENIUS"

Creating superb music required great creativity by a talented person. This special gift was often superimposed on top of what was an otherwise ordinary or conflicted life. Some of the most famous musicians who were considered "genius" often encountered the same human conditions that all the rest of us face. Reading about the lives of Mozart, Beethoven, Tchaikovsky, and Elvis Presley, I was struck by a common thread: their unhappiness as they tried to reconcile careers with the everyday pressures of real life.

Mozart was driven all through his life by the need for more income to finance an extravagant life-style, causing him to constantly seek new jobs and venues to increase his income. This was exasperated after marriage by a wife who was a spendthrift and wanted expensive things for herself and her family. They rode the rollercoaster up and down from wealth to poverty to wealth and back again.

The "genius" Beethoven was personally a most unpleasant, bearish guy you would not want for a next-door-neighbor or in your bridge group. Apparently his lady friends all discovered the same thing, because at least three of those he fell in love with and wanted to marry, rejected his proposals and married someone else. As a spurned suitor numerous times, he spent his entire life as an unhappy bachelor. It is also thought he may have suffered from a bi-polar condition.

Tchaikovsky endured an unhappy personal life distressed because of his homosexuality and trying to conceal it from his friends and the public. He married early in his career before he understood the situation and during the honeymoon encountered such a traumatic shock that he fell violently ill and spent weeks in recovery. During his lifetime at a time when homosexuality was not an understood or accepted condition, he lived (in the closet) in unhappy denial.

Elvis Presley, who made a profound impact on modern music, may not warrant the moniker of genius -- he was only a gifted performer, but in his later years he encountered a dysfunctional sexual life. After marrying a beautiful lady, he became unable to engage in sexual relations with her after the birth of their child; (alleged by her in a book) and sought sex with numerous other women, and ended his life in a deluge of drug abuse.

We hold these men on a pedestal of greatness, as well we should, because of the music they created that enhanced our lives; but fame left them with a downside in their personal lives as they struggled with some of the same day-to-day stresses ordinary people face. Perhaps we "non-genius" are more fortunate than the great ones: our lives are richer because of the music we inherited from them.

FORTY: DENOUMENT

In the Preface I talked about John Charles Thomas, a favorite singer of mine during the 1930's of my youth. Then in subsequent chapters I remembered other music: Puccini's opera *La boheme*, Tchaikovsky's *Fifth Symphony*, the Beatle's *Yesterday*, Frank Sinatra's *I Did It My Way*, and Barbara Streisand's *The Way We Were*.

Today, I am reminded of the great music of the yesterdays as I listen to a new sensation, pre-teenager soprano Jackie Evencho. She is an amazing talent even at her young age. What lies ahead for her in the world of music; will she become another great like Streisand?

I look forward in the years ahead to the wonderful world of music.

Bernie Keating

APPENDIX: TCHAIKOVSKY AND I

(From my 2010 book, *SONGS AND RECIPIES: For Macho Men Only.*)

Some of my favorite music was composed by Tchaikovsky. Shortly after Aurdery and I were married, we took a class together entitled Music Appreciation at a local college. The format was to focus each week on a piece of music in considerable detail and gain an appreciation for its musical development and why it had such a special impact on listeners. One of the "cause célèbre" was the Fifth Symphony of Tchaikovsky. During all the many years since, this musical work has been one of my favorites. The second movement in particular is one of the best in all of music.

Who can say why some particular piece of music has such a personal impact? I pondered this question and perhaps there is a connection between the orchestrated gyrations of this musical work and my work-a-day life in the glass factory. The music involves a long struggle, noise, repetition, complexity, controversy, and success ultimately at the end. The Fifth is a cyclical symphony, with a recurring main theme, which is heard in all four movements. It starts with a funereal character in the first movement, but gradually transforms into a triumphant march, which dominates to the end. The musical theme development is thought to experience "providence" -- divine guidance -- and expresses the idea of ultimate victory through strife. The other evening I was home alone. I put Tchaikovsky's Fifth on the stereo and sat down with a glass of wine. The music started. As my eyes glazed over, I found myself in a twilight zone somewhere between the music and days-gone-by; I was back again in the glass factory.

FIRST MOVEMENT: andante - allegro con anima. It is moderately slow and a ponderous statement, yet with vitality and excitement. I find it to be confusing: moderately slow and even; yet brisk, lively, sprightly, walking, and cheerful with animation. Yes, it is all those things in a mixed bag, much like my day of work in the glass factory. I am walking into the factory now. It is 6:30 a.m. as I am enveloped by the tumult of the factory: clanking of metal on metal of the bottle machines, blasts of compressed air, grinding of conveyor belts, whine of air fans, phones ringing, bottles clanking against each other; all in a rising crescendo -- trumpets come in as the recurring theme of "fate" goes over-and-over; now an octave higher. The B1 production shop roars as the bottles get dumped into a cullet chute. As I walk down the production lines, I see problems: machine problems, people problems -- my problems. I hear the harmonic overtones: trumpets, violas, oboes, bassoons, clarinets, and cellos -- all in dissonance-- piccolos barely discernible above the violins, and then the tympanis. The music grows faster and more energetic, but remains dark and apprehensive, occasionally punctuated by loud, violent outbursts. It is as if fate is coming after me with every foreboding, malevolent tool in its bag: union threats, uncontrolled costs, a strike, another mass worker layoff. At last I reach my office and close the door. I am in my safe sanctuary. The music fades as the movement come to an end.

SECOND MOVEMENT: andante cantabile, con alcuna licenza - moderato con anima. It starts slow and even, liberating, vital, liveliness, sprightliness, veracity, excitement, gay, songlike, flowing, and singing. The tender, haunting, expressive solo melody played by the French horn resonates with passion. Now I am retired, elderly, and living in comfort as I think again about those yesteryears in the glass factory. Things are going fine; at least for now. I cherish the fond memories of Ray, Charley, and Dick, and the comradeship we shared for so many years. Ed's funeral comes back to me with the haunting dirge of the French horn, underpinned with the deep baritone of the double bass played an octave lower and grumbling in counterpoint. Yes I am at peace with my memories.

Then suddenly my reverie is shattered as the music roars its turbulence as if fate is calling me back, and I am unable to escape my protagonist. I am again with the unrelenting roar of the glass factory; I am brought again to reality. The music rises in a crescendo, and slowly fades away.

THIRD MOVEMENT: valse, allegro moderate. The music starts with a graceful pastoral waltz and I am again in my sanctuary office with the door closed and slowly I read the mail. I have temporarily escaped from fate's cruel clutches. My secretary blocks the door and will re-direct all my phone calls. It is a moment of quiet and of peace. I quietly slip out my back door and head to the warehouse, and walk up and down the empty corridors with my mind elsewhere in a refreshing diversion from the cares of the factory. But there are musical overtones suggesting a quiet statement of the fate theme that is both innocuous and ominous. Try as I might, my protagonist-self cannot escape destiny. I return to my office and there sits Carlos -- the union president -- waiting for me. He is angry with me and with the company and with the world, and he lets me know in unmentionable terms. There is no accommodation, no compromise; only confrontation. The music reacts with a loud crash of cymbals, roll of the base drums, horns blaring; I can see the maestro on his podium, hair flowing, swinging wildly at the orchestra, and he brings the music to a close with unrelenting finality and angry arms.

FOURTH MOVEMENT: finale, andante maestoso - allegro vivace. Tchaikovsky transposes the fate theme from the dusky moody key of E Minor to the bright sunshine of E major in a majestic and stately walk through my yet-to-come years of retirement. Trumpets, flutes, and stings of the violin are singing to me. I am inside the glass factory as I wave goodbye to my secretary and walk through the exit door for the last time. It is as if Tchaikovsky is walking alongside and telling me that we cannot escape from our destiny; but can overcome my circumstances -- the hard work, the daily grind -- and turn them into something brighter and better. He gives me this universal theme through his music, and he is telling me it can be applied to my life. Just as his music is lifting me up and carrying me to new heights, I am reminded that fate is in my own hands.

The music comes to an end, but I remain with eyes closed and ponder again the musical friendship of Tchaikovsky and his symphony.

ENDNOTES

1. Carter Harman, *A Popular History of Music*, Dell Publishing Company, Inc, New York, 1956, pg. 11
2. "Music Psychology," *Wikipedia the free Encyclopedia 2011*
3. Pam Belluck, *New York Times Newspaper*, New York, NY, 4/19/2011
4. Harmon, op. cit., pg 15
5. "Ancient Music Traditions", *Wikipedia, op. cit.*
6. "Neolithic People", *Wikipedia, op. cit.*: The Neolithic Era was a period in the development of human technology, beginning about 9500 B.C. that is considered the last part of the Stone Age
7. "History of Europe", *Encyclopædia Britannica,* 2007 Deluxe Edition, Chicago
8. "Culture of Greece", *Wikipedia, op. cit.*
9. Harmon, op. cit., pg 17
10. "Architecture of Ancient Greece", *Wikipedia* op. cit.
11. "Architecture", *Collier's Encyclopedia*, P.F. Collier & Son, New York, NY, 1960, Vol. 2, pg. 82
12. "Homer", *Wikipedia, op. cit.*
13. Ibid.
14. "Music of ancient Rome, *Wikipedia*, op. cit.
15. "Pax Romana", *Wikipedia*, op. cit.: Pax Romana (Latin for "Roman peace") was the long period of relative peace and

minimal expansion by military force experienced by the Roman Empire in the 1st and 2nd centuries A.D. Its span was about 207 years (27 B.C. to 180 A.D.).

16.   Ibid.
17.   Ibid.
18.   Ibid.
19.   H.G. Wells, *The Outline of History*, Doubleday & Company, N.Y. 1961, pg. 412
20.   Ibid., pg. 506
21.   "Romanesque", *Encyclopædia Britannica*, op. cit.
22.   Ibid.
23.   "Romanesque", *Wikipedia, op. cit.*
24.   Ibid.
25.   Ibid.
26.   "Gothic Architecture", *Wikipedia, op. cit.*
27.   Ibid.
28.   Ibid.
29.   Ibid.
30.   Ibid.
31.   Ibid.
32.   Ibid.
33.   "Byzantine Empire," *Wikipedia, op. cit.*
34.   Ibid.
35.   Ibid.
36.   Ibid.
37.   "Renaissance", *Encyclopædia Britannica*, op. cit.
38.   "Renaissance," *Wikipedia, op. cit.*
39.   "95 theses", *Wikipedia, op. cit.*, The Ninety-Five Theses, was written by Martin Luther in 1517 and is widely regarded as the primary catalyst for the Protestant Reformation. The disputation protests against clerical abuses, especially the sale of indulgences.
40.   Ibid.
41.   "Renaissance Man", *American Heritage Dictionary. Definition:*

"Renaissance Man" is a man who has broad interests and is accomplished in areas of both the arts and sciences."

42. "Leonardo da Vince", Wikipedia, *op. cit.*

43. H.G. Wells, op. cit., pg. 606

44. "Humanism", *Wikipedia*, op. cit.

45. "Renaissance Art," Wikipedia, *op. cit.*

46. "Renaissance Art", *Encyclopædia Britannica*, op. cit.

47. Ibid.

48. "Renaissance Art," *Wikipedia, op. cit.*

49. "Venice", *Wikipedia, op. cit.*

50. Ibid.

51. Harman, op. cit., pg. 30

52. "Basso Continuo", *Wikipedia*, op. cit., a kind of integer musical notation used to indicate intervals, chords, and non-chord tones, in relation to a bass note. Basso continuo was used in almost all genres of music in the Baroque period, though rarely in modern music.

53. Ibid., pg. 32

54. Ibid., pg. 33

55. Ibid., pg. 34

56. Ibid., pg. 35

57. "Baroque", *Encyclopædia Britannica*, op. cit.

58. "Baroque", *Wikipedia*, op. cit.

59. "Architecture", *Colliers op. cit.*, pg. 84

60. Ibid.

61. "Shakespeare", *Wikipedia, op. cit.*

62. "Baroque", *Wikipedia, op. cit.*

63. Ibid.

64. Ibid.

65. "Bach", *Wikipedia*, op. cit.

66. Harman, *op. cit.*, pg. 41

67. "Bach", *Wikipedia, op. cit.*

68. "'Classic Period", Wikipedia, op. cit.

69. Ibid.

70. Ibid.

71.   Ibid.

72.   Ibid.

73.   "Mozart", *Wikipedia, op. cit.*

74.   Ibid.

75.   Harmon, op. cit., pg 135

76.   "Romanticism", *Encyclopædia Britannica*, op. cit.

77.   "Romantic Period", *Wikipedia, op. cit.*

78.   Ibid.

79.   Ibid.

80.   *Ibid., pg. 129*

81.   Ibid., pg. 244

82.   "Tchaikovsky", *Wikipedia, op. cit*

83.   Ibid.

84.   Ibid.

85.   Ibid.

86.   Modeste Tchaikovsky, *The Life and Letters of Peter Ilyich*

87.   *Tchaikovsky*, Vienna House, New York, 1906, Vol. 1. Pg. 287

88.   "Giccomo Puccini", *Wikipedia, op. cit.*

89.   Ibid.

90.   Ibid.

91.   Ibid.

92.   *Random House Dictionary of the English Language*, Random House, NY, 1970 *Leitmotif*: "Theme associated throughout a musical drama with a particular person, situation, or idea."

93.   "Jazz", *Wikipedia, op. cit.*

94.   "Jazz", *Collier's Encyclopedia*, op. cit., Vol. 10, pg. 648

95.   *"Jazz", Wikipedia, op, cit.*

96.   "Jazz", *Encyclopædia Britannica*, op. cit.

97.   *"Jazz", Wikipedia, op, cit.*

98.   Ibid.

99.   Ibid.

100.   Ibid.

101.   Ibid.

102.   Ibid.

103.   Ibid.

104. Ibid.
105. "Jazz", *Encyclopædia Britannica*, op. cit.
106. *"Jazz", Wikipedia, op, cit.*
107. "Louis Armstrong", Wikipedia, op cit.
108. "Louis Armstrong", *Encyclopædia Britannica*, op. cit.
109. "Louis Armstrong", *Wikipedia, op, cit.*
110. "Music", *Collier's Encyclopedia*, op. cit., Vol. 13, pg. 680
111. "Ibid., pg. 580
112. "Boogie Woogie", *Wikipedia, op. cit.*
113. Ibid.
114. "Boogie Woogie", *Encyclopædia Britannica*, op. cit.
115. *"Jazz", Wikipedia, op. cit.*
116. Ibid.
117. Ibid.
118. "Swing", *Encyclopædia Britannica*, op. cit.
119. "Jazz", *Collier's Encyclopedia*, op. cit., Vol. 10, pg. 650
120. *"Jazz", Wikipedia, op, cit.*
121. Ibid.
122. Ibid.
123. Ibid.
124. Ibid.
125. Ibid.
126. Ibid.
127. "Big Band", *Wikipedia, op. cit.*
128. Ibid.
129. Ibid.
130. Ibid.
131. "Glenn Miller", *Wikipedia*, op. cit.
132. Ibid.
133. Ibid.
134. Ibid.
135. "Glenn Miller", *Encyclopædia Britannica*, op. cit.
136. "Lawrence Welk", *Wikipedia,* op. cit.
137. Ibid.
138. "Lawrence Welk", *Encyclopædia Britannica*, op. cit.

139.   "Lawrence Welk", *Wikipedia, op.cit.*

140.   "Bebop", *Wikipedia, op. cit.*

141.   "Jazz", *Collier's Encyclopedia*, op. cit., Vol. 10, pg. 651

142.   "Bebop", *Wikipedia, op.*

143.   "Jazz", *Collier's Encyclopedia*, op. cit.

144.   "Rhythm and Blues", *Collier's Encyclopedia*, op. cit.

145.   "Rhythm and Blues", *Wikipedia, op, cit.*

146.   Ibid.

147.   Ibid.

148.   "Rhythm and Blues", *Encyclopædia Britannica*, op. cit.

149.   "Jitterbug", *Encyclopædia Britannica*, op. cit.

150.   "Jitterbug", *Wikipedia, op. cit.*

151.   Ibid.

152.   Ibid.

153.   Ibid.

154.   "Lindy Hop", *Wikipedia, op, cit.*

155.   Ibid.

156.   Ibid.

157.   Ibid.

158.   Ibid.

159.   "Folk Music", *Wikipedia, op, cit.*

160.   Ibid.

161.   Bernie Keating, *1960s DECADE OF DISSENT: The Way We Were*, Author House, Bloomington, IN, 2009

162.   "Marching Bands", *Wikipedia, op. cit.*

163.   Ibid.

164.   "John Philip Sousa", *Wikipedia, op, cit.*

165.   "Rock and Roll", *Encyclopædia Britannica*, op. cit.

166.   "Rock'n'roll", *Wikipedia, op, cit.*

167.   Ibid.

168.   Ibid.

169.   Ibid.

170.   "Elvis Presley", *Wikipedia, op, cit.*

171.   Ibid.

172.   Ibid.

173. Ibid.
174. Ibid.
175. Ibid.
176. "Country Music", *Wikipedia, op, cit.*
177. Ibid.
178. "Eddie Arnold", *Encyclopædia Britannica*, op. cit.
179. "Country Music", *Wikipedia, op. cit.*
180. Ibid.
181. Ibid.
182. "Country Music", *Encyclopædia Britannica*, op. cit.
183. "Willie Nelson", *Encyclopædia Britannica*, op. cit.
184. Ibid.
185. "Carry Underwood", *Wikipedia, op. cit.*
186. Ibid.
187. Ibid.
188. "Musical Theatre", *Wikipedia, op. cit.*
189. "Musicals", *Encyclopædia Britannica*, op. cit.
190. Ibid.
191. "Musical Theatre", *Wikipedia, op. cit.*
192. Ibid.
193. Ibid.
194. "Musical Theatre", *Wikipedia, op. cit.*
195. "Jackie Evencho" *Wikipedia, op. cit*
196. Ibid.
197. Ibid.
198. Ibid.